Practical Guide to Identifying Fake News, Scams and Biased Journalism in Your City

Copyright © 2024 Reginaldo Osnildo
All rights reserved.

PRESENTATION..5

WHY CARE ABOUT THE QUALITY OF LOCAL JOURNALISM? 9

FAKE NEWS IN LOCAL JOURNALISM - HOW TO DETECT FALSE OR DISTORTED STORYLINES................................16

SOURCES AND CHECKS - HOW TO CHECK THE AUTHENTICITY OF INFORMATION.................................25

RELEASES AS REPORTAGE - HOW TO IDENTIFY "COPY AND PASTE" JOURNALISM 34

OFFICIAL LANGUAGE - WORDS AND PHRASES THAT REVEAL DISGUISED RELEASES 43

SINGLE SOURCES AND OMISSION OF CONTEXT - WHEN THE RELEASE SPEAKS MORE THAN THE JOURNALIST ...53

OPINION COLUMNS AND ARTICLES - WHEN OPINION IS PASSED OUT AS NEWS 62

WORD CHOICE - POSITIVE TERMS AND EUPHEMISMS THAT SOFTEN REALITY 71

SELECTION CRITERIA - WHEN FACTS ARE SELECTED TO BENEFIT SOMEONE 80

ADVERTISING AND PAID MATERIAL - HOW TO IDENTIFY CONTENT THAT HAS BEEN PURCHASED.........................89

WHO'S PAYING THE BILL? ADVERTISERS' INFLUENCE ON IMPARTIALITY..97

"SPECIAL COVERAGE" AND "SPONSORED PROJECT" - SIGNS OF MANIPULATED CONTENT 105

AGENDA JOURNALISM - WHEN AGENDA REFLECTS POLITICIANS' INTERESTS 113

EDITING MANEUVERS - PHOTOS, TITLES AND HIGHLIGHTS THAT DIRECT PUBLIC OPINION 122

DISCREET COVERAGE OF LOCAL CRISES AND SCANDALS 131

SILENT OPPOSITION - WHY LOCAL JOURNALISM IGNORES CERTAIN GROUPS 139

DIFFERENT SOURCES AND CONTRASTING OPINIONS - HOW TO IDENTIFY A WELL-RECORDED STORY 148

EDITORIAL INDEPENDENCE - WHEN A NEWSPAPER OR BLOG REALLY TELLS THE TRUTH 157

CRITICAL QUESTIONS TO ASK WHEN READING A STORY 166

UNDERSTAND THE ROLE OF MAYORS AND COUNCILORS - THEIR FUNCTIONS AND RESPONSIBILITIES 175

CITIZEN RIGHTS - HOW AND WHERE TO QUESTION REPRESENTATIVES 184

THE POWER OF TRANSPARENCY - HOW TO HOLD POLITICIANS TO ACCOUNT 193

MUNICIPAL COUNCILS AND PUBLIC FORUMS - OPPORTUNITIES FOR PARTICIPATION 202

LOCAL ORGANIZATION AND ACTIVISM - UNITING THE COMMUNITY TO DEMAND IMPROVEMENT 210

USING SOCIAL MEDIA FOR TRANSPARENT COLLECTION 219

30 DAYS TO EVALUATE AND DEMAND ACTION FROM JOURNALISM AND LOCAL REPRESENTATIVES..............228

AN ACTIVE AND INFORMED CITIZEN TRANSFORMS HIS COMMUNITY..236

REGINALDO OSNILDO..242

PRESENTATION

Welcome to the book "**Practical Guide to Identifying Fake News, Scams and Biased Journalism in Your City**". This is a straightforward and practical guide for those seeking to understand how local journalism can impact their perceptions of politics and public life around them, revealing the subtleties and, at times, manipulations present in coverage of local issues.

In recent years, distrust of the media has become a central issue, especially in light of the rise in fake news and the proliferation of unreliable or manipulated information. We often hear about these problems on a national or international scale, but what about local journalism in our own city? Local media, despite being closer to citizens and having the potential to accurately report on essential issues affecting their daily lives, can also be vulnerable to pressure and influence, whether due to political interests or dependence on sponsors who influence the content broadcast.

This book is an invitation for you, as a reader and citizen, to become a more critical consumer of the information you receive, especially when it comes to local issues. In journalism, not everything that is published as news is, in fact, impartial. With a critical eye, it is possible to identify the signs of biased content, whether through press releases disguised as reports, the omission of relevant facts, or the use of words and euphemisms that soften reality. This type of critical perception is essential for us to be able to exercise our rights and, more than that, contribute to a better informed and fairer society.

The structure of the book was designed to guide you in a gradual and practical way. Throughout the chapters, you will find tips and tools to identify everything from fake news and subtle manipulations to sponsored articles and stories, often disguised as impartial reports. Each topic is explored in detail, offering techniques to help you question and validate the information. The idea is that, by the end of the book, you will not only have a better understanding of how local journalism works, but also know how to position yourself and demand more transparency and quality in the information that impacts your community.

This book, however, goes beyond criticism. It also provides a practical view of the role of city council members, mayors and other representatives, as well as guidance on how you can actively exercise your citizenship, demanding improvements and transparency from your representatives. Local journalism, when well executed, is an essential tool for social control and a powerful ally in building better cities. However, for it to fulfill its role, it must also be held accountable and monitored.

To help you on this journey, at the end of the book, we have prepared a 30-day action plan. With it, you will be able to evaluate and monitor the quality of journalism in your city, putting into practice the tools and strategies presented in each chapter. From monitoring local news and identifying sponsored stories, to direct contact with city council members and active participation in municipal councils and forums, this plan will provide you with practical experience of observation and citizen participation.

Remember: we are not here to attack the local media, but to encourage you to keep a vigilant and questioning eye. Ultimately, transparent and responsible journalism benefits society as a whole. May this guide be an ally in your quest for a more informed, fair and aware city. It is your right and your role as a citizen to understand what is happening behind the headlines, to question whenever necessary and to demand journalism that truly represents the interests of the community.

Happy reading and let's unmask and strengthen local journalism together!

Yours sincerely

Reginald Osnildo

WHY CARE ABOUT THE QUALITY OF LOCAL JOURNALISM?

Local journalism is uniquely important, yet it often goes unnoticed in everyday life. This type of journalism is not limited to reporting on events happening in your city, but has the potential to be a reflection of the community and promote transparency and public accountability. The role of local media is crucial in ensuring that society is aware of what is really happening around it and that everyone can make more informed and fair decisions.

However, local journalism does not always fulfill this role in an impartial and responsible manner. In many cases, political and commercial interests and proximity to authorities interfere in the way news is presented. The focus of journalism can be distorted to serve the specific interests of public or business figures, hiding problems, softening crises and manipulating the perception of reality. Therefore, understanding the importance of quality local journalism and learning to identify possible distortions is essential so that you, as a citizen, are not taken in by biased or manipulated news.

HOW LOCAL JOURNALISM INFLUENCES POLITICAL PERCEPTION IN YOUR CITY

Imagine that a city councilor recently elected to office has accumulated several allegations of financial irregularities, but the local media decides to cover this fact in a biased manner, highlighting only the positive side of his initiatives. By omitting or softening the issue, this coverage directly affects the community's perception of this public figure, influencing the next elections and the councilor's own performance. The quality of local journalism, therefore, directly affects the way the population understands and follows politics in their city.

This influence can be both positive and negative. Local journalism committed to ethics and truth can expose abuses, investigate allegations of corruption and question the actions of local politicians. On the other hand, biased journalism can reinforce support for authorities who manipulate information or who only seek their own interests.

THE IMPORTANCE OF RECOGNIZING SIGNS OF BIAS

At this point, it is important to understand what "bias" means in the context of journalism. When we talk about bias, we are referring to journalism that, whether intentionally or accidentally, chooses to cover events in a way that favors certain figures or institutions. Often, bias is not easily identifiable, as it manifests itself in details such as the choice of words, photos, or the way the news is structured. In some situations, it may be difficult to notice, for example, that an article is favoring an authority because, at first glance, it appears to present the facts in a "neutral" way. But upon closer inspection, you may notice that the tone of the report, the use of certain terms, and even the focus of the article reveal an intention to influence the reader's opinion.

To avoid being fooled by this type of bias, it is essential that you develop a critical eye for local media. And this means learning to question the source of each piece of information, and identifying and distrusting articles that treat certain topics superficially or that avoid addressing certain critical points. Throughout this book, you will find several tools to carry out this analysis in a practical way.

THE IMPACT OF INFORMATION MANIPULATION

Information manipulation is the act of directing news or omitting important parts of a fact to favor a particular image, opinion or public figure. In the context of local journalism, this practice can have a devastating effect, as it creates a distorted reality for residents, who begin to see the authorities and their actions through a manipulated lens. By creating a positive, false or exaggerated image of certain political figures or projects, local media can divert attention from real problems and make the population believe that everything is fine, when in reality there are crises and scandals being hidden.

This manipulation, which occurs mainly behind the scenes, is often subtle. It can be present in the choice of a title, in the editing of the interviewees' speeches, in the constant repetition of certain topics and the omission of others. As a result, the reader can be led to believe that a certain politician is always acting in favor of the community, while problems such as misappropriation of funds or neglect of duties are camouflaged or minimized.

Therefore, it is essential that you, as a citizen, learn to identify these practices so as not to be manipulated.

HOW YOU CAN MAKE A DIFFERENCE

By taking an interest in the quality of local journalism, you are taking an important step towards a more aware and informed society. Having a critical eye and knowing the tactics used to manipulate the news will allow you to become a careful monitor of the information you consume. This awareness is the first step to effectively questioning and demanding a fairer and more impartial press.

By following the local media with this more critical eye, you also become an active part in the transformation of journalism. When the community starts demanding fair coverage and transparency from the authorities, the press feels the need to respond to this demand. Your participation, questions and, if necessary, your criticism are essential to ensure that the media does not become a mere propaganda tool for the authorities, but rather a true reflection of the interests and reality of the community.

WHERE TO START?

You've probably come across a news story or article that seemed "too good to be true" or that was quickly debunked or challenged by other sources. If you haven't yet adopted the habit of questioning information, now is the perfect time to start. In the next chapter, we'll look at how to identify fake news in stories that seem, at first glance, reliable and well-written. But before we go any further, here's an exercise: how about reviewing the latest articles you've read about local politics? Was there any news that seemed to favor a particular politician or institution? This type of initial analysis is an excellent step toward developing a critical and alert reading style.

Throughout this book, we will unravel several practices that distort journalism, such as publishing articles copied from press releases, selecting words that soften reality, and omitting context that diverts attention from problems. You will have access to practical methods for investigating the veracity of a news story, identifying whether it is based on real and diverse sources, or whether it simply repeats the version presented by some local authority without questioning it.

This book is more than a guide; it is an invitation for you to actively participate in building a more transparent, fair and responsible media. Each chapter will provide not only examples and explanations, but also practical exercises so that you can apply this knowledge in your daily life, strengthening your capacity for critical analysis.

By completing this first chapter, you have already taken an important step in questioning the quality of local journalism and preparing yourself to identify potential manipulations. This is the beginning of a journey of awareness that will allow you to see beyond the headlines and actively participate in monitoring the actions of your representatives and demanding a local press committed to the truth.

FAKE NEWS IN LOCAL JOURNALISM - HOW TO DETECT FALSE OR DISTORTED STORYLINES

Fake news is no longer a new phenomenon in the communications world. Since the emergence of social media, the term has gained prominence and has come to be associated with false, exaggerated or manipulated information that spreads quickly and can cause serious harm. Although it is often seen as a national or global phenomenon, fake news also operates locally and affects the way people perceive public figures, policies and even the safety of their communities.

In local journalism, fake news takes on more subtle forms and is therefore often accepted without question by the reader. It can manifest itself in small distortions of data, exaggerations to favor a public figure or omissions of relevant information, which end up diverting the focus from the real problems. For example, a mayor who inaugurates an unfinished project may be praised as an "efficient and dedicated authority", and criticism of this inauguration may be completely omitted in certain media outlets. This type of distortion creates a false perception and makes citizens believe in a manipulated reality.

THE FAKE NEWS CYCLE AND LOCAL JOURNALISM

The process of creating and spreading fake news usually follows a well-structured cycle. First, information with the potential to generate engagement — be it a controversial inauguration, a popular proposal, or a controversy involving local public figures — is created or altered to favor or harm someone. Then, this information is shared by smaller media outlets or independent websites, which reproduce the content without thoroughly verifying it. Soon, it gains an air of legitimacy, being republished by local newspapers that do not carry out rigorous fact-checking. This cycle can then transform false information into something widely accepted and disseminated.

This process is even more intense in small towns, where access to information is restricted and often monopolized by a few media outlets. In such places, verification of sources is neglected, and news can circulate without question, quickly becoming "truth" for the local population. A distorted news story about a local authority, for example, can solidify an image that affects everything from public trust to the next municipal elections.

HOW TO IDENTIFY SIGNS OF FAKE NEWS IN LOCAL JOURNALISM

Below, we will discuss the main signs that can help you detect fake news or distorted articles, even when they seem official and well-presented. Remember that, with practice, these signs become easier to identify and you will be able to develop a critical eye for the news you consume.

1. Check the source of the news

The first step to identifying fake news is to look at the source of the news. Check whether the article comes from a reliable website with a history of impartiality and commitment to the truth. Unknown sources or those with a questionable reputation deserve extra attention, especially if they publish sensationalist content or present major scandals without consistent evidence.

Even when the publication is well-known, it is essential to check whether the article mentions official and reliable sources. Be wary of texts that contain vague statements, such as "sources close to us" or "experts say", without providing details about who these sources are. This type of language may indicate that the news is based on rumors or dubious information.

2. Analyze the structure of matter

One of the most common characteristics of fake news is its appealing and sensationalist structure. Exaggerated headlines, impactful phrases and superlative adjectives are some of the elements that indicate the intention to manipulate the reader's emotions. When an article uses terms such as "scandal", "surprising" or "shocking" in an exaggerated way, this may be a sign that the news is aimed more at engagement than at providing real information.

Also, pay attention to the way the text is structured. Real, well-researched news stories usually have a balanced structure, with information that follows a clear line of reasoning. Fake news stories tend to be fragmented, with logical leaps and a lack of detailed data. This type of structure is a way of "covering gaps" in the information, because by presenting the facts in a confusing way, the text makes it difficult to understand and hides the lack of research.

3. Identify exaggerations and generalizations

Another characteristic of local fake news is the use of exaggerations and generalizations to inflame public opinion. Statements such as "the entire population is outraged" or "the mayor is solely responsible for all the problems" are signs that the article may be manipulating information. In serious journalism, journalists try to avoid generalizations, seeking to represent different points of view and presenting concrete evidence to support their statements.

When you come across an article that uses this type of exaggeration, question the veracity of the statements. A good practice is to look for alternative articles on the same topic to see if other sources also confirm the same version of the facts. This will help you have a more balanced view and avoid falling into manipulation traps.

4. Note the use of citations and sources

Fake news often distorts or invents quotes to give the news story more credibility. It is common, for example, to find articles that put words in the mouth of a local authority or an anonymous source, when in reality that quote was not said. An example of this would be an article that quotes an "expert" saying something controversial, without identifying the person's name or credentials. Another common practice is to present a quote out of context, which completely changes the meaning of what was originally said.

In local journalism, this can happen in a disguised manner, with statements from authorities or public figures being published without the necessary verification. When reading a news story that includes quotes, check whether the text provides clear information about the source and whether the quote is in line with the context of the article.

5. Be wary of agendas that divert focus from real problems

Fake news can also serve to divert the community's attention from real problems, redirecting the focus to less important or fabricated issues. Instead of covering important issues, such as the use of public resources, problems in education or health, some news outlets prefer to focus on stories that promote a positive image of public figures or bring up irrelevant topics. This can happen, for example, in the midst of a scandal, where positive news about a local authority is intensively circulated to drown out the problem and influence public opinion.

This type of strategy, known as a "smoke screen," is a sign of manipulation and deserves careful observation. If you notice a secondary issue being heavily promoted to the detriment of an important issue, ask yourself whether it is an attempt to divert attention from the real issues.

6. Check the temporality and originality of the news

Fake news often uses outdated or debunked information to create a misleading context. Sometimes, old news is republished as if it were recent to give a public figure a bad image or to reignite a controversy. When reading an article, check the date and see if there is any indication that the information has been covered before. Checking the timeliness prevents you from believing content that does not correspond to current reality.

Additionally, whenever possible, look for the news in other sources. Many fake news stories are copies of manipulated news stories that circulate on sensationalist websites or social networks without verification. If the news story has not been published in reliable media outlets, this is a strong indication that it may not be true.

PRACTICAL EXERCISE: DETECTING LOCAL FAKE NEWS

To reinforce the concepts covered, let's do a practical exercise. When reading the next news story about a local public figure, go through this checklist:

1. **Identify the source of the material** : is the vehicle known and reliable?
2. **Analyze the title** : is it sensationalist or exaggerated?
3. **Check the sources** : Does the news story cite reliable and identifiable sources?
4. **Look at the context** : is the focus of the news diverted to an irrelevant topic?
5. **Check the date** : is the article recent or is it republishing old content?

This checklist will help you identify the main signs of information manipulation and develop a critical view of local news.

Identifying fake news in local journalism is a crucial skill in an age where information circulates quickly and can be used to manipulate public opinion. By paying attention to details and questioning sources, you protect yourself against attempts to influence your perception and contribute to a more informed and aware community.

SOURCES AND CHECKS - HOW TO CHECK THE AUTHENTICITY OF INFORMATION

Verifying the authenticity of information is an essential practice in news consumption, especially in the context of local journalism, where the same source is often cited repeatedly without question. In some situations, a news story may seem true and even convincing, but when we investigate the sources, we discover that the information has been manipulated, exaggerated or simply based on rumors. This practice of verification is even more important in small towns, where access to news often comes from a limited number of outlets and the influence of local public figures on these outlets can be more direct.

Imagine, for example, an article that praises the city government's increased investment in infrastructure. Without verification, the reader may believe that the city is, in fact, growing and modernizing. However, when analyzing the sources and data, one may discover that these investments are limited or directed to areas that favor third-party interests. This example highlights the value of a critical eye to verify whether the information is reliable and whether there is a correspondence between the facts and what is being reported.

In this chapter, we will explore practical and accessible methods for checking the authenticity of news, examining the origin of sources, and recognizing when information has been manipulated to further a specific agenda.

STEP BY STEP TO VERIFY A NEWS STORY

1. Identify the sources mentioned

The first step to verifying the authenticity of a news story is to look at the sources cited. Reliable news stories usually clearly indicate their sources, which may be authorities, institutions, studies or experts. When a story relies on anonymous sources, does not present specific data or makes vague statements, this may be a sign that the information has not been properly researched.

For example, an article that states "experts say the mayor has broad approval ratings" without indicating who those experts are or what research supports that claim may be using a generic source to lend credibility to dubious information. Whenever you come across a quote from "sources close to you" or "experts say," question why the author didn't specify who those people or organizations are.

A useful practice here is to try to locate the original source of the information. If the article mentions a survey or study, look for the original document or consult reputable websites to confirm the existence of the study and verify the data. This helps ensure that the news story was not based on a selective or biased interpretation of the data.

2. Check that the sources are independent and diverse

One of the best ways to assess the quality of a news story is to analyze the diversity of sources. In journalism, especially when it comes to political and social issues, it is essential that stories present diverse perspectives, including both official sources and independent voices. When a news story relies exclusively on a single source, especially a government source or one directly linked to the featured figure, there is a greater risk of bias.

For example, a story that discusses improvements in public safety but only cites statements from the city government may fail to mention the real experiences of the population or civil society organizations involved. To ensure balanced coverage, the journalist should also seek the opinions of independent experts, representatives of security NGOs, or even reports from affected residents.

To conduct a critical analysis, check to see if the article presents different points of view on the topic. If you notice that only one perspective is being offered, this may indicate a biased view or an attempt to manipulate the reader's perception.

3. Confirm the data and statistics

Many fake or distorted news stories use manipulated data and statistics to reinforce an idea or support an opinion. Therefore, when you come across an article that uses numbers to support arguments, it is important to check the veracity of this data. In articles about the local economy, security, health and infrastructure, numbers can be used to legitimize a specific narrative, but when taken out of context or presented selectively, they distort reality.

To verify the authenticity of the data, look for the original sources of the statistics. Many data on the economy and local development, for example, can be found on official websites, such as the transparency portals of city governments, the Brazilian Institute of Geography and Statistics (IBGE) or state departments. By comparing the numbers presented in the article with the data from these sources, you will be able to identify any attempts at exaggeration or omission.

A common example is the publication of infrastructure investment figures that include funds that have not yet been released, giving the impression of a larger budget than is actually the case. By checking with official sources, you can find out whether these figures actually correspond to the approved budget and whether they are actually applicable to the city.

4. Evaluate the context and temporality of the news

Presenting news out of context can completely change the way we understand the facts. Local news stories often use data or events out of context to suggest improvements that are, in reality, temporary or superficial measures. For example, a story that praises the creation of new health clinics in the city may omit the fact that many of them are understaffed or have limited hours of operation. This type of decontextualization masks the real problems and creates a distorted positive image.

Another aspect to consider is temporality. Old news may be republished as if it were current, or a fact may be portrayed as recent when, in fact, it has already been corrected or clarified. To avoid this type of mistake, always check the publication date and, if possible, do a quick search to identify articles related to the same topic, which will allow a more complete and accurate view of what is really happening.

5. Analyze the tone and language used in the article.

The language of a news story can say a lot about its authenticity and impartiality. Serious news stories tend to adopt a neutral and objective tone, presenting facts without making judgments or using unnecessary adjectives. However, biased or distorted news stories often use appealing language, with adjectives and expressions that seek to manipulate the reader's emotions.

Pay attention to superlative terms and exaggerated statements, such as " never before seen," "exemplary," or "a historic victory" in articles about inaugurations of local works or projects. These terms may indicate a positive bias that aims to magnify the public figure in question. Likewise, a news story that demonizes a group or an idea using negative expressions such as "irresponsible," "absurd," or "harmful" deserves to be analyzed with caution, as this type of language is characteristic of articles that seek to influence the reader.

A useful trick to identify this manipulation is to imagine the same news being written in more neutral language. This helps you understand how the choice of words influences the perception of reality and assess whether the news is truly objective.

TOOLS AND SOURCES FOR VERIFYING INFORMATION

Below are some practical tools you can use to efficiently perform information verification:

- **Google News** : When you search for a news story on Google News, you can check whether other reliable sources have also covered the same topic. This helps confirm the authenticity of the information and prevents you from believing in exclusive, unverified stories.
- **Fact-checking sites** : Platforms such as Aos Fatos, Lupa, and Fato ou Fake are dedicated to verifying the veracity of information and rumors. Although they are focused on national news, these sites can be useful for checking data that may be used in a distorted way in the local context.
- **Transparency portals and government websites** : For information on budgets, security, health and education data, the transparency portals of city halls and state governments are reliable and accessible sources.
- **Consultations on public documents** : In many cases, it is possible to request access to public documents to obtain more detailed information about projects, contracts and budgets. The Access to Information Law (LAI) guarantees that any citizen can request this type of document.
- **Official social media** : Checking the official social media accounts of government agencies or political figures can help confirm the authenticity of statements and verify whether a quote is true. However, it is important to remain skeptical, as information can be manipulated even in official sources.

PRACTICAL EXERCISE: INVESTIGATING A LOCAL NEWS STORY

To exercise your fact-checking skills, choose a news story about your city and follow this process:

1. **Identify the sources mentioned in the article** : Are they reliable and clearly specified?
2. **Check the data and statistics** : Are the numbers presented confirmed by other sources?
3. **Analyze the context** : Is there anything omitted that could distort the understanding of the facts?
4. **Observe the language** : Does the news story use emotional or superlative expressions?

Performing this exercise regularly will allow you to develop a habit of critical analysis and strengthen your ability to distinguish facts from manipulated narratives.

Verifying sources and data is an essential practice to ensure that you are well informed and protected from manipulation. By developing the habit of questioning news, you become a more informed reader and less susceptible to the pitfalls of journalism that may be distorted by local interests.

RELEASES AS REPORTAGE - HOW TO IDENTIFY "COPY AND PASTE" JOURNALISM

" Copy- and-paste journalism" refers to the practice of publishing, virtually unedited, official statements, known as press releases, sent by government agencies, companies or press offices. This type of content is created with the intention of promoting a favorable image of an event, project or public figure, and often ignores critical aspects or presents a one-sided view of the situation. When a media outlet publishes these releases as if they were impartial reports, the news coverage is distorted, as the content ceases to be an independent analysis and becomes almost a reproduction of propaganda.

In the context of local journalism, copy- and-paste is even more common. Many media outlets face financial and staff constraints, which leads them to adopt press releases as a quick and practical way to generate content. For city and city council press offices, this practice is a valuable opportunity to project a positive image and direct the public narrative without questioning. Thus, copy - and-paste journalism becomes a dangerous cycle, where the public ends up receiving biased and manipulated information as if it were independent and reliable news.

In this chapter, we'll explore the signs that help identify the use of press releases as stories, understand why this practice is problematic, and learn methods to confirm whether a story is based on a press release or whether it is a truly verified story.

HOW TO IDENTIFY A RELEASE DISGUISED AS NEWS?

1. Writing style and promotional tone

Press releases are usually written in a positive and optimistic tone, with the aim of highlighting achievements and creating a favorable image for the public. When a media outlet adopts an unedited press release, it is common for the article to take on a promotional tone, praising the public figure or the project in question. If you read a news story that seems overly complimentary and lacking in critical information, consider the possibility that it is a press release.

Watch out for expressions such as "another great achievement", "historic result" or "exemplary efficiency" in the description of a mayor or council member's actions. These expressions aim to build a positive image, omitting difficulties or criticisms. When you notice this type of language, question whether the article presents a balance between the pros and cons of the action discussed. In a genuine report, even if there is praise, the journalist will usually also include some point of analysis or consideration, unlike a press release that only presents the idealized version.

2. Lack of multiple sources and perspectives

In investigative journalism, it is common for a report to include different sources to provide a balanced view of the topic. In contrast, a press release is limited to promoting the view of the organization or figure that wrote it, rarely addressing critical points or consulting external sources. For example, a press release about the inauguration of a public works project may omit the fact that the construction was delayed, had an increase in costs or was not carried out according to the initial plan.

One way to spot a press release masquerading as a report is to see if the article mentions only one source — usually the city government itself, a city council member, or the interested party. If there are no statements from residents, independent experts, or members of the opposition, it is likely that the article is based on a press release. Independent journalism always seeks to bring together a diversity of voices and perspectives, while press releases are often one-sided.

3. Structure of matter and repetition of data and expressions

The structure of a press release tends to follow a standard formula, starting with a brief, positive introduction, followed by details about the project or action, and ending with a favorable quote from a spokesperson. When a report reproduces this format verbatim, including repeated expressions or phrases identical to the official release, it is an indication that the journalist did not do their own research and simply copied the text.

When reading an article that follows this model, compare the structure and expressions with those published on the official websites or social media of the aforementioned organizations. If the news published by the local media outlet is identical or very similar, it is almost certainly a case of copy and paste.

4. Use of official jargon and technicalities

Releases often contain technical language and specific jargon, common in political or administrative discourse. Terms such as "management efficiency", "optimized urban mobility", "well-spent public resources" and "governance goals" are expressions often used to build a positive image, without clarifying exactly the impact of the actions.

When a news story adopts this language without adapting or questioning it, it is possible that the text is a literal reproduction of the press release. Journalism, in general, seeks to translate "bureaucratic jargon" into language that is accessible to the public, while copy and paste maintains the original language, which makes it difficult for readers to critically understand it.

5. Lack of questions and absence of context

One of the clearest signs that a story is based on a press release is the absence of questions about what is being reported. In a real news report, the journalist does not just disclose information, but investigates and seeks to clarify details that may impact the population. If a mayor announces the construction of a new school, for example, an investigative report would address issues such as the costs involved, the delivery time and the need for that work for the community.

On the other hand, a story that reproduces the press release simply reports the announcement without adding context or clarifying aspects that may be problematic. This type of story is characterized by "accepting" official information without any critical analysis, which is a dangerous practice for journalistic credibility.

PRACTICAL EXAMPLES TO IDENTIFY DISGUISED RELEASES

To illustrate these concepts, let's imagine two local news scenarios, one based on a press release and the other on a more complete report.

1. **Scenario 1: Opening of a new health unit**
   - **Release**: The article begins by praising the city government's efficiency in "offering yet another quality service to the population" and presents statements by the mayor about "the commitment to the health of all citizens." There is no mention of the cost of the project, the number of doctors available, or the expected impact on local health.
   - **Full report**: Includes residents' views on the need for the unit, questions the budget allocated and compares the service capacity with other health units in the region. The journalist also seeks to understand the future challenges of the unit to ensure that it meets the needs of the population.
2. **Scenario 2: Improvement in the public transport system**
   - **Release**: The text describes the measure as an "innovative initiative" and "a step forward for urban mobility," with quotes from city officials praising the improvement. There is no analysis of the difficulties faced by the current system, nor a projection of how the change will benefit the population.
   - **Full report**: Investigates the problems faced by the public transport system before the change, interviews users to find out what they expect from this improvement and includes the opinion of experts on the effects of the new policy.

In these examples, it is possible to notice that the press release omits crucial information and adopts a positive tone without questioning, while a true report offers a broad view and considers both the benefits and the difficulties of the initiative.

THE IMPACT OF COPY AND PASTE JOURNALISM ON THE COMMUNITY

Reproducing press releases as if they were genuine reports has a profound impact on society, as it deprives the public of the right to complete and balanced information. When a media outlet limits itself to publishing press releases, it abdicates its responsibility to investigate, question and inform in depth. For readers, this means having access to a one-sided view, which can omit problems and distort reality, generating a mistaken perception about public management and the quality of services offered.

This practice is even more damaging in small towns, where there are few media outlets and often a close relationship between the media and local authorities. When journalism stops questioning official information, it becomes a mouthpiece for the authorities and loses its role as a watchdog for the interests of the population. This results in a less informed community that is more vulnerable to political manipulation.

HOW TO REACT WHEN DETECTING A RELEASE DISGUISED AS A REPORT?

When you realize that a news story is based on a press release, you can adopt some practices to have a more complete view of the topic:

1. **Look for other sources** : Search for the same news story in other outlets to see if there are additional details or different perspectives.
2. **Check the official website** : Often, the release is available on the website of the city hall or the agency mentioned. By comparing the two versions, you can see if there was any copy and paste.
3. **Exercise your right to question** : Contact the media outlet and ask if the content was investigated or if it was based on the official release. This practice, when done respectfully, encourages journalistic transparency.

Copy -and-paste journalism is a common but dangerous practice that turns official press releases into supposed news stories and deprives the community of truly investigative journalism. By learning to spot the signs of a press release masquerading as a report, you become a more critical and aware reader, capable of questioning the information you receive.

OFFICIAL LANGUAGE - WORDS AND PHRASES THAT REVEAL DISGUISED RELEASES

The language used in a journalistic text can be as revealing as the facts themselves. In the context of local journalism, many apparently informative texts use "official" language that hides intentions of self-promotion and manipulation. The use of specific terms, administrative jargon and phrases that reinforce a positive image of authorities or public bodies can be an indication that the article was not written independently, but based on an official release, and is often an attempt to influence readers' perception of a politician, project or public initiative.

Official language is carefully chosen to create a favorable impression, creating an idealized scenario that highlights "achievements" and "advances" while omitting challenges, failures, and criticisms. This chapter will teach you how to identify these expressions and terms that reveal the presence of disguised press releases. By developing this skill, you will be better able to critically evaluate news and avoid being influenced by texts that seek to manipulate your perception.

WHY DO RELEASES USE OFFICIAL LANGUAGE?

Press releases are produced by communications teams that aim to promote a positive image for their clients — be it an authority, a government agency or a company. To do so, they use a set of terms and expressions that aim to soften criticism, extol qualities and attribute success and efficiency to the institution's actions. When this official language is used directly in a news article, without analysis or questioning, it creates biased content that, instead of providing balanced information, acts as a public relations tool for the figure or entity in question.

Local newspapers, often due to lack of resources or time, end up republishing these press releases without substantial changes, which results in articles full of complimentary terms that favor the authority. Understanding how these terms operate is the first step to identifying them and questioning the impartiality of the articles you read.

COMMON WORDS AND EXPRESSIONS IN THE OFFICIAL LANGUAGE

Below are some words and expressions frequently used in official press releases to create a positive image. Recognizing these terms is essential to identify when a text is trying to manipulate the reader's perception:

1. "Modernization" and "innovation"

These words are used to convey the idea that local government actions are forward-thinking and progressive. When a project is described as "innovative" or "part of the city's modernization," the text suggests that the authority is ahead of its time, making significant improvements to the community. However, these expressions are often used to disguise routine actions or improvements that are, in fact, mandatory, such as basic infrastructure renovations.

For example, when reading an article about the "modernization of public transportation", ask yourself if there is specific data that proves the improvement and if the innovation is really bringing concrete benefits to users.

2. "Commitment to the population"

The expression "commitment to the population" is common in political speeches and press releases that aim to reinforce the image of an authority as someone dedicated and concerned with the well-being of citizens. However, this expression is rarely accompanied by specific actions that prove this commitment.

When you come across this sentence, look for concrete examples that support the statement. A text that talks about "commitment to the population" when opening a school or health center should also provide information about the budget, the expected operating time, and the challenges faced during the process.

3. "Positive impact" and "transformation"

These expressions are used to suggest that a particular action has brought significant changes to the life of the community. Although they may seem complimentary, they often lack real evidence that the impact was, in fact, positive or transformative.

For example, an article describing a development project as a "transformation for neighborhoods" should provide data or accounts from residents that prove this change. The absence of practical examples and public opinions may indicate that the expression was used to create a positive impression without any basis in fact.

4. "Significant results" and "goal achieved"

These terms often appear in press releases that seek to demonstrate efficiency and success in projects or policies. Expressions such as "goal achieved" and "significant results" suggest that the authority or public body is effective and delivering on its promises. However, these goals are often vague or have easy-to-achieve criteria, which makes the "success" less impressive than the text makes it seem.

To question these expressions, check whether the text presents specific numbers or describes the goals clearly. An example of checking would be to compare the results presented with data from previous periods, which helps to identify whether there has really been an improvement or if the results are just average.

5. "Pioneering initiative"

This term is used to suggest that an action is unique or innovative, highlighting the authority as a "leader" who introduces something new to the community. In practice, "pioneering initiative" can be an empty term, used to describe something that has already been implemented in several other cities or that is not really innovative in nature.

When you come across this expression, ask yourself: are there really no other similar initiatives? Researching other sources or looking for examples from other cities can help you see if the term is just used for self-promotion.

6. "Strategic partnership"

The expression "strategic partnership" is common in press releases that want to convey the idea that the public agency or political figure is carrying out intelligent and collaborative management, partnering with other entities to obtain benefits. However, this expression usually omits the costs involved, the interests of the partners and the challenges of implementing this partnership.

When reading about a "strategic partnership," look for information about the type of agreement established, the commitments of each party, and the real expectations of benefits to the community. This critical analysis allows you to look beyond the optimistic language and understand the real impact of the partnership.

PRACTICAL EXAMPLE OF IDENTIFYING THE OFFICIAL LANGUAGE

Let's look at a fictional example of a story and identify the signs of official language:

Article : "In yet another pioneering initiative, our city's government, committed to the well-being of its population, has opened a new leisure center. The initiative is part of the city's modernization program, which aims to have a positive impact on residents' quality of life. According to the mayor, the leisure center is a reflection of the administration's commitment to achieving significant results and meeting goals."

In this matter, we can observe several expressions of official language:

- "Pioneering initiative" suggests that the opening of the leisure center is something unique and innovative, but the article does not explain why the project is pioneering.

- "Commitment to the well-being of the population" is a vague and non-specific expression, which reinforces the positive image of the mayor without offering details on how the leisure center meets this commitment.
- "Positive impact on quality of life" suggests a broad benefit, but the article does not provide data to prove this impact.
- "Significant results and goals" create a sense of efficiency and success, but there is no description of which goals were achieved or how the leisure center contributes to these "results".

When reading an article with these characteristics, it is essential to question the authenticity of the statements and look for information that proves the benefits and relevance of the action.

STRATEGIES FOR IDENTIFYING AND QUESTIONING OFFICIAL LANGUAGE

When you come across a news story that uses expressions typical of official language, you can adopt the following strategies to assess whether the article is truly impartial:

1. **Replace vague expressions with concrete questions** : When you read phrases like "commitment to the population" or "significant results", ask yourself "commitment in what way?" or "what results were achieved?" This practice

allows you to see if the article is lacking specific details.
2. **Compare the article with other media outlets** : If the news is based on a press release, it is likely that other media outlets will publish similar texts. Checking for identical repetitions of the same expressions in different local newspapers is a good indication that the content may have originated from an official statement.
3. **Research independent sources** : Try to find articles or commentaries from experts, academics, or even community members that offer an independent perspective on the topic at hand. This can help you verify whether the impacts presented actually correspond to reality.
4. **Note the lack of concrete data** : One of the main characteristics of official language is the lack of specific data. If an article uses a lot of positive expressions without including numbers, user reports or other concrete details, it is probably based on a press release.

The official language used in press releases and reproduced without criticism in local reports is a subtle way of manipulating public perception. By learning to identify these expressions and questioning the use of vague and complimentary terms, you become able to analyze information more clearly and demand journalistic coverage that is truly committed to the truth.

SINGLE SOURCES AND OMISSION OF CONTEXT - WHEN THE RELEASE SPEAKS MORE THAN THE JOURNALIST

One of the fundamental principles of journalism is a commitment to impartiality and accuracy, which usually involves listening to multiple sources and presenting a context that allows the reader to understand the news in a broad and balanced way. However, in local journalism, many stories are published based on a single source — often an authority or public body — and without adequate context, which results in a biased and often manipulated view of the facts.

Using only one source, without seeking counterpoints or contextualization, creates an imbalance in the journalistic narrative. In this scenario, the content ceases to be complete information and becomes a monologue that favors the central figure or entity of the news. The absence of multiple perspectives or critical contextualization prevents the reader from understanding the different sides of a topic, causing them to see the news from a limited perspective that is often favorable to specific interests.

In this chapter, we will explore how to identify articles with unique sources or with omission of context and how to develop a critical reading to evaluate the quality of the information you consume.

WHY IS USING A SINGLE SOURCE A PROBLEM?

By basing a story on a single source, a journalist misses the opportunity to present a complete and balanced picture. Using multiple sources allows the story to include different perspectives and give the reader a deeper understanding of the facts, especially when the topic is controversial or involves political interests.

When local journalism relies exclusively on authorities, such as mayors, city council members or advisors, without hearing other sides, it risks becoming a spokesperson for these figures, rather than a critical and impartial observer. In health stories, for example, the city government may report on an advance in medical care, but without consulting patients or specialists, the story omits the real experience of users and the technical opinion of those who know the health system. This type of approach distorts reality and can create an unrealistically positive image.

HOW TO IDENTIFY THE USE OF A SINGLE SOURCE

1. Check for multiple voice citations

One of the easiest ways to identify the use of a single source is to look at the statements or quotes in the article. In a well-researched report, it is common to find opinions from multiple stakeholders—government officials, residents, experts, critics, and members of the opposition. When an article presents only the views of one official body or politician, it is a clear indication that there was no attempt to seek a balanced view.

For example, in a news story about a new public project, the journalist could include the opinions of people affected by the project, the position of opposition councilors and, if relevant, the views of urban planning experts. The absence of these voices indicates that the story was constructed to reproduce only the point of view of the authority involved.

2. Notice if there are "ready-made answers" or superficial speeches

When a story is based on a press release, the statements or statements made by the authority are often generic and not very substantial. These ready-made responses are characteristic of a story that has not undergone a more in-depth journalistic investigation process. In committed journalism, the journalist questions, investigates and demands more details from their sources, avoiding publishing vague statements or unsubstantiated self-praise.

When reading an article that cites a single authority, question whether the statements are truly informative or whether they seem like standardized responses. Statements such as "our commitment is to quality of life" or "this project will transform the city" are indicative of a narrative without depth, which only aims to promote the image of the public figure.

3. Identify the absence of counterpoints

One of the clearest signs of using a single source is the lack of counterpoints. In an article that addresses controversial topics or involves public issues, counterpoints are essential to provide the reader with a critical view. When the article does not provide counterpoints or divergent opinions, the reader does not have access to a balanced view and may be led to accept the information as "absolute truth."

Imagine a news story about a public transport fare increase that only provides the city government's justification without hearing the opinions of users or the opposition. By omitting these voices, the journalism does not allow the reader to understand the real impacts of the decision and ends up favoring the authority's version without any dispute.

4. Question the origin of the source

In local journalism, it is common for official sources to be cited without providing details about their role or possible interests. When reading an article that cites only one source, ask yourself who that person is, what their position is, and what interests may be behind their statement. Identifying the origin and role of a source allows you to better understand the weight and motivation behind that information.

For example, if the article quotes an "expert" without providing further details about his or her field of expertise or connection to the authority in question, be suspicious. Often, figures with political ties or commercial interests are presented as "experts" to lend legitimacy to the authority's view, but their impartiality may be questionable.

THE OMISSION OF CONTEXT AS A FORM OF MANIPULATION

The omission of context is another strategy used to influence readers' perception. Context is the set of additional information that allows the reader to understand what is behind an action or decision. Without this context, the news becomes superficial and does not reveal the details that could help the public understand the impact of what is being reported.

Omission of context occurs, for example, when a city hall announces a project as "unprecedented" without mentioning that other similar attempts have failed in the past or that the project involves a high and unforeseen cost. This omission creates a perception that the action is innovative and positive, without making clear the history and risks involved.

HOW TO IDENTIFY THE OMISSION OF CONTEXT

1. Compare with other sources

One of the best ways to spot a lack of context is to compare the story to other news stories on the same topic. If a city government announces the creation of a new health service, for example, look for other sources to see if there is additional information. More complete coverage will usually include data on the cost of the project, the number of beneficiaries, and any implementation difficulties, while a story without context will only mention the announced benefit.

2. Look at the theme's history

Another way to identify the lack of context is to consider the history of the topic being discussed. When a city faces recurring problems, such as lack of water, security or infrastructure, any action to solve these problems should mention the history of previous attempts. An article about a new investment in public safety, for example, should mention previous investments and assess whether they actually brought improvements.

When reading a news story that omits the history of an issue, the reader may believe that the new action will solve the problem immediately, without knowing that similar measures have already been tried and failed in the past. This type of omission is a way to manipulate public perception and avoid criticism.

3. Question the absence of negative impacts

News stories that omit context often fail to mention potential negative impacts of the announced actions. If a story about the construction of a new road presents only the infrastructure and development benefits, but does not mention potential environmental impacts or the cost to the community, this indicates that context has been intentionally omitted to avoid critical thinking.

When you come across news that seems "too good to be true," ask yourself what the potential challenges or side effects of that action might be. The absence of negative aspects is often an indication that context has been omitted to manipulate public perception.

PRACTICAL EXERCISE: IDENTIFYING SINGLE SOURCES AND CONTEXT OMISSIONS

To practice your critical analysis, do a practical exercise with a news story from your city:

1. **Read the news and identify the sources** : Who was interviewed? How many sources were interviewed? Were there counterpoints?
2. **Seek additional context** : See if other articles on the same topic provide additional information or historical data that help you understand the action in more depth.
3. **Analyze the presence of negative impacts** : Does the article present negative points or challenges? If not, question whether they were omitted on purpose.

These steps will help you identify whether the story provides a complete view or is limited to a one-sided, partial perspective.

The use of single sources and the omission of context are practices that weaken local journalism and reduce the quality of information available to the public. These practices turn articles into disguised propaganda, which favors authorities or public bodies by omitting important data and avoiding counterpoints. By learning to identify these characteristics, you become a more attentive reader and less susceptible to manipulation.

OPINION COLUMNS AND ARTICLES - WHEN OPINION IS PASSED OUT AS NEWS

Journalism is a powerful tool for shaping opinions, especially on topics of public interest. However, for journalism to be truly informative, it is essential that it clearly distinguishes between facts — objective information based on evidence — and opinions — subjective interpretations and points of view. In local journalism, this distinction is not always respected, and the opinions of columnists or journalists are often presented as if they were facts, biasing the reader's perception.

Columns and opinion pieces are legitimate spaces for expressing views, but they must be clearly identified and separated from objective news. When this line is blurred, readers can be led to believe that an opinion piece—often favorable to a government official or action—is an objective description of reality. This type of distortion affects public understanding and weakens readers' ability to form their own opinions based on data and balanced perspectives.

In this chapter, we will explore how to identify opinion pieces disguised as news, understand the function of columns and editorials, and develop tools to assess whether information is objective or expresses a personal point of view.

THE FUNCTION OF COLUMNS AND OPINION ARTICLES IN JOURNALISM

Columns and opinion pieces are spaces dedicated to commentary and personal analysis of relevant topics. Unlike news reports, which seek objectivity and neutrality, these texts reflect the interpretation and judgment of the person who writes them, whether a columnist, journalist or guest. In transparent journalism, opinions are identified and separated from news so that the reader can distinguish between personal interpretation and objective facts.

However, in many small towns where local media have close ties to public figures and authorities, opinion columns can be used as a disguised form of propaganda. Instead of critical analysis, these pieces present highly favorable views of government actions or political figures, attempting to influence the reader to adopt a particular viewpoint. When this occurs without a clear separation between opinion and fact, the credibility of the information is compromised.

HOW TO IDENTIFY WHEN AN OPINION IS PASSING OUT AS NEWS

1. Check the title and tone of the text

One of the quickest ways to spot an opinion piece disguised as news is to look at the headline and the tone of the text. Opinion headlines often use adjectives and expressions that reveal a personal view, such as "excellent initiative," "exemplary management," or "ideal solution." The tone of the text also tends to be more emphatic and personal, with the use of emotional expressions or value judgments, such as "unacceptable," "brilliant," or "regrettable."

For example, an article titled "Mayor shows competence in opening new school" already conveys a favorable opinion, suggesting that the action is worthy of praise. In an objective report, the title should simply inform the fact, such as "Mayor opens new municipal school", leaving it up to the reader to interpret the competence or impact of the action.

2. Observe the use of subjective expressions

In opinion pieces, it is common to find subjective expressions that reflect the author's personal judgment, such as "unfortunately", "fortunately", "it is clear that" or "everyone agrees that". These expressions reveal that the text is more focused on convincing the reader of a specific view than on presenting the facts impartially.

For example, if a news article states that a new traffic policy "will hopefully bring more order to the city's streets," the use of "fortunately" indicates a positive outlook. This type of expression conveys a personal view, suggesting that everyone should view the policy as beneficial. In impartial journalism, the article would present the policy's objectives and the opinions of different groups, allowing the reader to form their own judgment.

3. Analyze whether the text presents other points of view

A legitimate opinion piece does not necessarily have to present multiple points of view, since its purpose is to defend a specific perspective. However, when a piece disguised as news only adopts a favorable or unfavorable view, without listening to other sides, this indicates that it may be promoting an opinion as if it were fact.

An article about a city hall project, for example, should include diverse opinions, such as those of experts, residents and representatives of the opposition, in case these groups are affected or have criticisms to make. The lack of multiple perspectives limits the reader's view and encourages the acceptance of the author's opinion as the only truth.

4. Question the presence of excessive praise or one-sided criticism

Another clear sign that an opinion piece is masquerading as news is the use of excessive praise or one-sided criticism. Pieces that exaggerate the qualities of an authority or strongly condemn a group without presenting concrete evidence and data are generally not objective reports.

For example, a news story that describes a mayor as "tireless in the fight for the well-being of the population" or that defines criticism from the opposition as "unfounded and irresponsible" is using an opinionated and biased tone. Objective journalism avoids such emotionally charged judgments and focuses on describing the facts.

5. Look for the author's signature or identification

In general, opinion pieces are written by columnists, commentators or journalists, while objective reports are more common in articles written by the editorial staff. If a text includes the author's name followed by "columnist" or "editorialist", this indicates that it is an opinion piece. However, when the text is not identified as an opinion piece and still contains subjective judgments, it is disrespecting the separation between information and personal interpretation, which can confuse the reader.

When you come across an unsigned article that presents a vehement favorable or unfavorable view, question the impartiality of the content. If the newspaper has not indicated that it is an opinion, this may indicate an attempt to pass off a personal perspective as news.

THE DIFFERENCE BETWEEN EDITORIALS AND REPORTS

Editorials are a specific type of opinion piece published by media outlets to express the newspaper's official position on a given topic. Unlike news reports, which seek to be impartial, editorials are deliberately opinionated and reflect the institution's point of view. Although they are legitimate, editorials must be clearly identified so that the reader knows that they are reading an opinion piece and not a news story.

However, in some local newspapers, the line between editorial and reporting is blurred, and editorials may be published as news stories, favoring a public figure or government policy without providing counterpoints. This distorts the function of journalism, as the reader is led to believe that the editorial's viewpoint is a factual description of events.

PRACTICAL EXAMPLE OF AN OPINION DISGUISED AS NEWS

Let's analyze a fictitious example:

Article : "In yet another demonstration of his commitment to the city, Mayor José Silva has demonstrated efficiency and vision by inaugurating the new sports center. The initiative, which already has the support of most residents, represents an important step for local youth. Everyone recognizes that this administration is bringing significant improvements."

In this example, we can identify several signs of disguised opinion:

- "Proof of commitment" and "efficiency and vision" are subjective expressions that suggest a positive evaluation of the mayor's actions.
- The statement that "most residents support" the initiative is generalizing and does not provide data to support this statement.
- "Everyone recognizes that this management is bringing improvements" is a statement that lacks proof, suggesting that the author's view represents the general opinion.

This article, instead of offering objective journalistic coverage, presents a personal view that promotes the image of the mayor, trying to influence the reader to see the action as positive without presenting critical arguments.

PRACTICAL EXERCISE: EVALUATING A NEWS STORY TO IDENTIFY DISGUISED OPINION

To develop your ability to identify opinions disguised as news, do the following exercise:

1. **Read a news story about a local topic** and check the tone of the headline and content. Is there praise or veiled criticism?
2. **Look for subjective expressions** : Try to identify adjectives and terms that indicate a judgment, such as "important", "necessary", "regrettable" or "competent".
3. **Check for multiple sources** : Are there differing opinions? Does the text present statements from different sides of the issue?
4. **Compare with other news** : Read other articles on the same topic and see if there is a consensus or if the outlet seems to be presenting a very specific view.

This exercise will help you recognize when a text is disguising an opinion and avoid being influenced by content that does not provide a balanced view.

Confusing opinion with news weakens journalism and compromises the reader's ability to form an informed opinion. By learning to identify opinions disguised as news, you become a more critical reader and able to distinguish between personal interpretations and objective facts.

WORD CHOICE - POSITIVE TERMS AND EUPHEMISMS THAT SOFTEN REALITY

Word choice is a powerful tool in journalism and has the potential to significantly influence a reader's perception of a news story. In local journalism, where authorities often have a close relationship with the media, the use of positive terms and euphemisms can be a strategy to soften problems and present a more favorable reality than the situation actually requires. By opting for language that minimizes or camouflages difficulties, local journalism fails to fulfill its critical function and begins to contribute to the creation of a narrative that favors certain public figures or actions.

Euphemisms are expressions that make an idea or fact less impactful or negative, softening the weight of the information. When used in news articles, they change the way the reader understands and reacts to the news, promoting a more positive view of topics that, in practice, would deserve a more detailed or critical analysis. In this chapter, we will examine how to identify these terms and expressions, understand why they are used, and develop strategies to "translate" these words into a more objective language that is closer to reality.

WHY IS THE USE OF EUPHEMISMS A COMMON PRACTICE?

In the context of local journalism, the use of euphemisms and positive terms is a common practice to avoid conflicts and criticism directed at local authorities, such as mayors, councilors and municipal secretaries. To maintain a "harmonious" relationship with these figures, many media outlets opt for less critical words that soften flaws, avoiding terms that could have a negative impact and harm the image of the administration.

For example, a "health budget reduction" could be described as a "strategic cost review," diverting the reader's attention from the possible negative impacts of such a reduction. This strategy encourages the perception that local government actions are always positive, even when, in reality, they harm the population.

HOW TO IDENTIFY EUPHEMISMS AND POSITIVE TERMS THAT SOFTEN REALITY

1. Watch out for the use of vague and generic terms

Vague terms such as "improvements," "adjustments," "optimization," and "streamlining" are often used to describe changes that in practice amount to cuts, reductions, or limitations in public services. These terms create the impression that the actions are beneficial or necessary without directly addressing the potential negative effects on the community.

For example, a news story that says the city will make "adjustments to school infrastructure" may be hiding the fact that these adjustments include closing schools or reducing maintenance investments. Vague terms leave room for a positive interpretation and prevent the reader from understanding the true impact of the action.

2. Identify expressions that soften problems

Expressions such as "temporary hardship," "challenging situation," or "fiscal adjustment" are often used to soften serious problems. Instead of describing a problem clearly and objectively, these expressions seek to minimize the situation, leading the reader to believe that the issue is temporary or less serious than it really is.

Imagine a news story about a hospital facing a shortage of basic supplies. If the story describes the situation as a "temporary hardship," it softens the issue and prevents the reader from understanding the severity of the impact on public health. A more direct approach would describe the shortage of supplies as a real risk to medical care, encouraging the reader to question the causes and solutions to the problem.

3. Pay attention to the use of motivational and encouraging terms

When a news article describes an action as "an important step" or "a strategic decision for the future," it may indicate an effort to promote a positive image of unpopular or risky decisions. Motivational terms like these are especially common in topics such as infrastructure, economics, and public administration.

For example, a news story about the sale of public land to investors might be described as "a strategic decision to boost local development." This word choice creates the perception that the sale will benefit the city, but it omits the fact that the community will lose a public space. The motivational word choice distracts from the risks and favors an optimistic view.

4. Recognize the use of euphemisms for financial problems

Financial euphemisms are common in local journalism, especially when it comes to deficits, budget cuts or tax increases. Expressions such as "realignment of resources", "fiscal adjustment" and "tax modernization" soften the impact of financial actions and try to reduce the reader's negative perception.

A practical example is an article that announces "adjustment of municipal taxes" instead of clearly stating that tax or service rates will be increased. The expression "adjustment" softens the impact, preventing the reader from perceiving the action as an additional financial burden. Understanding these expressions and questioning them helps to identify the true financial effect on the population.

5. Be wary of terms that suggest control or stability

When a difficult situation is described with terms such as "control," "responsible management," or "balance," the text is trying to convey the idea that the situation is under control and that there is no need to worry. These terms are used to reinforce the image that the local government has control over the problems and is acting efficiently.

Imagine an article describing a spike in violence as "a security challenge under control." This term creates the impression that the problem is being addressed, even though the violence data suggests otherwise. Using words like "control" and "balance" diminishes the perception of risk, leading the reader to believe that the issue is under the control of authorities, even without clear evidence.

STRATEGIES TO AVOID BEING INFLUENCED BY EUPHEMISMS AND POSITIVE TERMS

Below are some practices that help identify and challenge the softening of issues through the use of euphemisms in local journalism:

1. **Mentally translate euphemisms** : When you come across vague expressions like "resource optimization" or "fiscal adjustment," ask yourself what the reality behind the phrase is. Often, these terms mean cuts in services, tax increases, or other measures that can directly impact the population. Train your eye to translate euphemisms into more direct terms.
2. **Compare with other articles and sources** : Check whether other media outlets or alternative sources are covering the same topic in more direct language or whether they provide data and statistics that can debunk the euphemism. Often, news from independent portals or local social networks can provide details that are ignored by traditional media.
3. **Research the history of the topic** : If a measure is described with words like "modernization" or "reorganization," look for information about the history of that action. Have similar actions been carried out in the past? Has there been a positive impact or has the measure resulted in criticism? Analyzing the history allows you to understand the real meaning of the terms used and predict possible impacts.
4. **Question the lack of specifics** : Euphemisms often replace clear facts and detailed information. If a story talks about "strategic partnerships" without describing the terms of the deal or the costs involved, this could be a sign that something is being sugarcoated. A lack of specific details is a sign

that the word choice is glossing over sensitive points.
5. **Notice the impact of word choice on the tone of the story** : Analyze the overall tone of the story and notice how word choice influences the final impression. A story filled with positive terms and euphemisms creates a sense of control and success, even though the actual facts may be less than favorable. This practice of "embellishment" is a form of subtle manipulation.

PRACTICAL EXERCISE: IDENTIFYING EUPHEMISMS IN A LOCAL STORIES

To practice analyzing euphemisms, choose a news story about a controversial topic in your city, such as budget cuts, adjustments to public services, or partnerships with private companies. Then do the following:

1. **List the softened words and expressions** : Write down the terms that seem to soften or make the situation more positive, such as "modernization", "adjustment", "strategic partnership".
2. **Search for alternative meanings** : Look for information on the topic in other sources and try to "translate" the euphemisms into more direct and realistic words.
3. **Question the impact on the population** : Ask yourself what the concrete impacts of the action described are and how the use of euphemisms may

be hiding important information or negative effects.

This exercise will help you develop a more critical reading style that is less influenced by word choices that seek to manipulate perception.

The use of positive words and euphemisms in local journalism is a strategy used to soften issues and promote a more favorable image of public figures or actions. This practice diverts the reader's attention from information that could raise questions or concerns, constructing a convenient narrative that does not always reflect reality. By learning to identify and translate these euphemisms, you become more aware of the real impacts of political decisions and actions in your community.

SELECTION CRITERIA - WHEN FACTS ARE SELECTED TO BENEFIT SOMEONE

Journalism is, at its core, a fact-finding activity. When writing a story, a journalist must decide what information to include, what angles to explore, and how to present the data. However, this fact-finding process must follow ethical principles, seeking impartiality and a commitment to the truth. When the fact-finding process is distorted to emphasize certain facts and omit others, the final narrative becomes biased and can lead the reader to adopt a specific view, often favorable to a public figure or authority.

In local journalism, where journalists tend to be more closely associated with public figures, cherry-picking is a common strategy for avoiding criticism or for building a positive image of authorities. By emphasizing events, accomplishments, and statements that favor a public figure or agency, local journalism can convey an impression of progress and efficiency while omitting flaws, criticisms, and challenges that would give readers a more complete and honest view. In this chapter, we will explore how to identify biased fact-picking and develop skills to recognize when a story is manipulating context and presentation of information.

HOW FACT SELECTION INFLUENCES PUBLIC PERCEPTION

Fact-picking is a subtle technique that can profoundly influence a reader's perception. Imagine, for example, a story about a city's public health management. If the story focuses only on improvements, such as the acquisition of new equipment or the opening of health facilities, and omits data on chronic problems, such as a shortage of doctors or increased waiting times, the reader will get the impression that the health system is in good condition. This selective choice creates a narrative of success and efficiency, diverting the focus from problems and criticisms that should also be addressed.

Another common example is when a newspaper highlights successes or positive events that occurred under the administration of a mayor or city council member, but ignores scandals, protests or problems that arose at the same time. This type of intentional selection directs the public's attention to a specific and convenient aspect of reality, hiding information that could weaken the image of the authority. This type of manipulation is harmful because it restricts the public's ability to understand the real situation, evaluating only one part of the story.

HOW TO IDENTIFY FACT SELECTION IN LOCAL STORIES

1. Note the absence of negative or critical contexts

One of the first signs that an article is using a selection of facts to favor someone is the absence of negative or critical context. When reading an article about a government action or public policy, ask yourself if the text presents any data that allows for a critical analysis of the action. A balanced article usually includes not only the positive aspects, but also the challenges and difficulties faced by the initiative.

For example, a news story about the revitalization of a public park might describe the financial investment and infrastructure improvements, but it should also address issues such as environmental impacts, timeliness, and resident reactions. The absence of these aspects indicates that the journalist may be cherry-picking facts, favoring a positive view.

2. Analyze whether the article prioritizes statements from a single source

When a news story relies primarily on statements from a single official or official without hearing other voices, it is likely that the selection of facts is biased toward that official's view. In stories involving local government actions, ethical journalism should seek out a variety of sources—such as experts, community members, and opposition representatives—to provide a balanced view.

If the article only contains statements from an authority or person involved in the project, this limits the reader's critical perception. More impartial coverage would listen to diverse opinions, such as those of citizens affected by the action and independent experts. This allows the reader to have access to a more complete and realistic view.

3. Check for excessive focus on secondary events and actions

In some cases, a story may emphasize minor or secondary events and achievements, diverting attention from more significant issues. For example, a local newspaper may devote a lengthy story to the opening of a small cultural center, highlighting the presence of officials and the investment made, while omitting serious and more impactful issues, such as the lack of investment in security or health.

This type of selection focuses on events that build a positive image of the administration, while more critical and relevant issues for the population are left aside. If you notice very detailed coverage of secondary actions or events, ask yourself whether other more urgent issues are not being omitted.

4. Identify when the article ignores history and comparisons

One way to manipulate readers' perceptions is to omit historical action or comparative data that would allow them to assess whether there has been a real improvement or progress. For example, an article about a new public safety program might describe the program as a "significant step forward," but omit information about failures in previous programs or data that would allow them to compare the situation before and after implementation.

When reading an article about a new project or policy, ask yourself whether the text mentions similar actions taken previously and whether it presents comparisons with data from previous years. This allows you to assess whether the new action actually represents an improvement or whether it repeats past problems.

5. Be wary of articles that ignore important data and statistics

The omission of data and statistics is another form of subtle manipulation in journalism. Journalists often avoid presenting numbers when such data could undermine the positive view they are trying to convey. A story about local economic growth, for example, might omit information about unemployment or rising living costs that would give a more realistic view of the situation.

To identify this practice, check whether the article presents statistics that support the claims made. If not, seek independent sources to verify whether the data corresponds to the scenario being described. The absence of numbers in articles that deal with quantitative topics, such as the economy, health and infrastructure, is a sign of fact-cherry-picking.

ANALYSIS EXERCISE: IDENTIFYING THE SELECTION OF FACTS IN A NEWS STORY

To practice fact-selection analysis, choose a recent news article about a topic relevant to your city and ask yourself the following questions:

1. **Is there any critical or negative context missing from the story?** Ask whether the news presents challenges, difficulties or negative impacts that could balance the view presented.
2. **Does the article prioritize a single source?** See if there are statements from different sources or if the text prioritizes only one authority.
3. **Does the text focus on secondary actions or events?** Notice if the article presents minor actions as if they were of great importance, diverting the focus from more urgent issues.
4. **Is there history and comparisons?** Check whether the article presents the history of the action and compares it with data from previous periods.
5. **Are statistics and data included?** Ask whether the article presents relevant numbers and data to provide an objective view.

Answering these questions allows you to identify whether the article is providing a complete and balanced view or whether it is a cherry-picking of facts to manipulate the reader's perception.

WHY IS FACT SELECTION HARMFUL?

The selection of facts is a form of manipulation because it distorts reality and creates a narrative that is convenient for authorities and public figures, limiting the reader's understanding of the real situation. This practice prevents the population from fully evaluating the actions of local managers and makes it difficult to form an informed opinion. In a democracy, access to accurate and impartial information is essential for society to be able to exercise its role of oversight and accountability.

When local journalism adopts fact-picking as a recurring practice, it becomes an ally of political interests, failing to fulfill its role as a watchdog of society and a guarantor of public transparency. This practice also generates distrust among the population, who begin to question the credibility of local media and lose a reliable source of information.

Fact-picking is a subtle but powerful strategy that can profoundly influence public perceptions of government and government actions. By learning to recognize when facts are being cherry-picked to favor a positive view and by questioning the absence of context and data, you can develop a critical eye and avoid being manipulated.

ADVERTISING AND PAID MATERIAL - HOW TO IDENTIFY CONTENT THAT HAS BEEN PURCHASED

Paid articles, also known as " advertorials " or " advertisements ," are sponsored content published in media outlets that present a positive view of a product, service, or public figure. This type of content is legitimate and common, but it needs to be clearly identified so that the reader knows that it is not impartial news but rather an advertisement. However, in local journalism, this distinction is not always made transparently. This can confuse the reader, causing them to interpret an advertisement as an objective report.

When paid stories are not properly flagged, they act as a disguised form of manipulation, promoting a positive image of specific companies, politicians or projects, without the reader realizing the commercial or political interest behind the content. In this chapter, we will explore how to identify paid stories and understand why this practice undermines transparency and trust in local journalism.

THE FINE LINE BETWEEN REPORTING AND ADVERTISING

Paid articles become a problem when they are presented as news reports, without any indication that they are sponsored content. This type of article seeks to convince the reader that the information was independently researched, when in reality it was funded to highlight specific qualities and omit critical points. The line between advertorial and news report becomes blurred, and the reader may be led to believe a biased or exaggerated view, without knowing that it was paid for by someone interested in promoting it.

Imagine, for example, that a city hall pays a local newspaper to publish an article about a new housing project, praising its benefits and citing only statements from authorities. If the article is not marked as paid, the reader will understand it as an impartial report, when in fact it was financed to promote a positive image of the project and public management. This type of practice is ethically questionable, as it uses the newspaper's credibility to sell an image, without transparency for the reader.

HOW TO IDENTIFY A PAID ARTICLE

Here are some tips for identifying whether a story may be sponsored, even when there is no explicit notice:

1. Note the lack of visual and textual identification

The first way to identify a paid article is to check if there is any visual or textual identification that indicates that it is sponsored content. In ethical journalism, paid articles are usually marked with terms such as " advertorial ", "sponsored content" or "offered by [name of company or institution]". This identification must be clear and visible, usually positioned at the beginning or next to the title.

If you don't see this identification and notice that the tone of the text is extremely favorable or promotional, be suspicious. The absence of a formal notice does not mean that the content is not paid, especially if the tone is overtly complimentary or if there is a lack of critical analysis.

2. Analyze the overly positive or promotional tone

Paid articles often have a more enthusiastic and complimentary tone than objective reporting. Phrases such as "this transformative initiative", "an innovative solution for the city" or "an example of competence and efficiency" are common in advertorials . This type of language is more characteristic of advertising than of journalism, which tends to be more neutral and balanced.

For example, a story that describes a new city service as "essential to the well-being of all residents" may be a paid piece. Independent journalism would use more neutral language, presenting the action without offering unsubstantiated praise. If the tone seems enthusiastic and biased, this could be an indication that the story was sponsored.

3. Note the absence of counterpoints or independent sources.

A common characteristic of paid articles is the lack of counterpoints and independent sources. The text usually only contains positive statements from figures associated with the project or service in question, without mentioning challenges, criticisms or opinions from experts who are not linked to the sponsored content. When an article is limited to complimentary statements from the responsible authority, it is reproducing a positive narrative without offering in-depth analysis or criticism.

For example, a paid news story about an infrastructure project might only quote statements from officials and contractors, without including the opinions of independent engineers or residents of the affected area. The absence of other sources indicates that the story is trying to promote a one-sided and controlled view, characteristic of sponsored content.

4. Identify repetitive and detailed mentions of brands, figures or projects

A clear sign that a story may be paid for is the repeated and detailed use of the name of a brand, public figure or project. Advertorials usually seek to reinforce the name of the sponsor to promote recognition and associate the brand or figure with a positive image. In journalism, it is common to use generic terms to refer to a company or authority after mentioning it once, but in sponsored content the name is repeated frequently.

For example, in a paid article about a mayor, the mayor's name may be mentioned repeatedly, followed by praise or mention of positive actions. This indicates an attempt to cement the name of the sponsor or authority in the reader's mind, a practice more associated with advertising than with journalism.

5. Be wary of content published on strategic dates

Another sign of paid content is the publication of content that praises public figures on strategic dates, such as pre-election periods, important events in the city or inaugurations of public works. Local authorities often sponsor content to coincide with their agendas, taking advantage of high-profile events to strengthen their image in the community.

For example, a series of stories about "administration accomplishments" in the week leading up to an election could be a sign that the content was commissioned to influence voters. Pay attention to the context of the publication and ask yourself whether the content could be serving a specific purpose to promote an authority or party.

PRACTICAL EXERCISE: INVESTIGATING A SUBJECT TO IDENTIFY IF IT IS PAID

To practice identifying a paid article, choose a news story about a project or public figure in your city and follow these steps:

1. **Look for visual and textual identification** : Check if there is any clear notice that the content is sponsored.
2. **Analyze the tone and language** : Is the tone overly positive? Is there a lot of praise without critical support?
3. **Look for other sources** : Does the article present independent perspectives or is it limited to sources directly related to the topic?
4. **Note the repetition of names** : Is the name of the figure or institution mentioned repeatedly? Is there an attempt to reinforce the image of the sponsor?
5. **Consider the publication date** : Does the publication coincide with an event, an inauguration or an election period?

Answering these questions helps you develop a critical eye to identify sponsored content disguised as reporting.

WHY IS TRANSPARENCY ABOUT ADVERTISING IMPORTANT?

Transparency is a fundamental value in journalism, as it allows readers to differentiate between an investigative and impartial report and an advertisement . When a media outlet fails to indicate that content is sponsored, it undermines the credibility of the journalism and confuses the public, who then interpret the content as reliable news. This undermines citizens' right to clear and honest information, which is essential for them to make informed decisions about local and political issues.

Furthermore, the lack of transparency regarding paid articles reinforces the perception that local journalism is at the service of specific interests, rather than the community. In a democratic context, it is essential that the public be able to distinguish between independent journalism and advertising in order to exercise its role of monitoring and criticizing the authorities.

Paid articles or advertorials are common and have legitimate value in the communications market, but they need to be clearly identified so as not to mislead the reader. By learning to identify these contents, you become a more attentive reader and able to differentiate between advertising and independent journalism, avoiding being influenced by disguised propaganda.

WHO'S PAYING THE BILL? ADVERTISERS' INFLUENCE ON IMPARTIALITY

Local journalism plays a crucial role in informing the community about events and decisions that affect citizens' daily lives. However, this role can be compromised when news outlets become dependent on large advertisers—especially when those advertisers are local officials, politicians, or companies with interests in public policy. By relying financially on these sponsors, local newspapers may find themselves under pressure to tone down criticism, avoid negative coverage, or even promote a favorable image of their sponsors.

This dependence creates a conflict of interest that compromises the impartiality and credibility of journalism. When commercial needs override the commitment to truth, local journalism ceases to fulfill its oversight function and becomes a public relations tool for its sponsors. In this chapter, we will understand how the influence of advertisers affects journalistic content, how to recognize this interference, and what you, as a reader, can do to assess the impartiality of the stories you consume.

HOW ADVERTISERS INFLUENCE NEWS CONTENT

Advertisers with significant financial clout can exert direct and indirect influence over the content published by media outlets. In some cases, the influence is explicit: advertisers demand that their actions be reported only in a positive light or that topics that could harm their image be avoided. In other cases, the influence is subtle, manifesting itself in self-censorship on the part of the editorial staff, who prefer not to publish criticism so as not to jeopardize the sponsorship that sustains the newspaper.

Imagine, for example, that a large construction company that finances advertisements in a local newspaper is the target of criticism for the quality of a public project. If the newspaper depends financially on this company, it may choose not to cover the issue or to tone down the story, omitting negative aspects and highlighting only the positive impacts of the project. In this way, the reader receives an incomplete version of the facts and ends up being deprived of the right to accurate and critical information.

HOW TO IDENTIFY THE INFLUENCE OF ADVERTISERS ON ARTICLES

1. Notice overly positive coverage of certain advertisers

When a newspaper devotes a disproportionate amount of content to promoting a single company, official or agency, this may be an indication of advertiser influence. Reports that repeatedly extol the qualities and achievements of a specific public figure or company, without providing counterpoints or criticism, suggest that the newspaper is favoring the advertiser in question.

For example, if you notice that a local newspaper frequently publishes complimentary articles about the actions of the city government or a company that is an advertiser, this may indicate a relationship of dependence that influences the editorial content. The consistent positive tone may be a way to please the sponsor and ensure continued financial support.

2. Identify the absence of reviews or investigations on important advertisers

One of the clearest signs of advertiser influence is the lack of investigative or critical reporting on topics directly related to the advertiser. When a newspaper avoids covering scandals, management issues, or community criticism involving a company or authority, it is likely that the sponsor is interfering to avoid negative publicity.

For example, if a large local company faces labor or environmental complaints and the newspaper does not publish any article about it, or only covers the topic superficially, this indicates that the outlet is avoiding criticizing the sponsor. This selective silence prevents readers from learning about real problems and compromises the transparency of journalism.

3. Notice the use of promotional language when mentioning the sponsor

The use of promotional language when referring to a sponsor is another indicator of influence. In an impartial report, journalism uses neutral and descriptive language. However, when a newspaper refers to advertisers with complimentary and superlative adjectives — such as "innovative," "visionary," or "exemplary" — this may be a sign that the content was influenced by an interest in maintaining a favorable relationship with the sponsor.

For example, if the local newspaper consistently describes a public transport company as "efficient" and "committed to quality", even when there are complaints from the public about the service, it is possible that the complimentary tone was shaped to please the sponsor and avoid conflict.

4. Note the presence of advertising integrated into the articles

When a newspaper is funded by influential advertisers, it is common for it to integrate advertising elements into its articles. This can take the form of subtle mentions of the sponsor's services or products, images and logos inserted into reports, or even direct quotes from spokespeople who praise the qualities of the company or authority. This type of practice turns journalistic content into a disguised advertising piece.

For example, a story about a cultural fair sponsored by a company might include repeated mentions of the sponsor's name and praise for its "commitment to local culture," rather than simply reporting on the event. This type of integration of editorial content and advertising confuses the reader and undermines the objectivity of the news story.

5. Question the exclusivity of topics covered and the constant focus on advertisers' projects

If a media outlet frequently covers the same projects, actions and figures linked to sponsors, neglecting topics of public interest and independent figures, this may be a sign of advertiser influence. This intentional selection of topics creates an exclusive focus on sponsors, leaving aside subjects that could provide a more complete view of local reality.

For example, if a newspaper always covers the urban development projects of a construction company that is an advertiser, but does not address problems such as the lack of schools or hospitals, this may indicate that the outlet prioritizes the interests of the sponsor over the public interest.

PRACTICAL EXERCISE: ASSESSING THE INFLUENCE OF ADVERTISERS ON A STORY

To develop your ability to identify advertiser influence, choose a story about a local company or public figure and do the following analysis:

1. **Count how many positive stories about the sponsor were published** : Notice if there is a disproportionate amount of stories praising the sponsor compared to other local figures or topics.
2. **Look for criticism and counterpoints** : Does the article present any criticism or counterpoint? If not, ask whether the newspaper is avoiding addressing negative aspects.
3. **Evaluate the language** : Check to see if the text uses promotional adjectives or overly complimentary language.
4. **Identify advertising integration** : Does the content repeatedly mention the brand or the sponsor's qualities? Is there integration between editorial content and promotional elements?
5. **Examine the range of topics** : Does the newspaper cover topics of general interest or does it focus too much on topics related to the sponsor?

Answering these questions allows you to assess whether the article was influenced by the interest of maintaining a good relationship with the advertiser or whether it presents an independent view.

THE IMPACT OF ADVERTISERS' INFLUENCE ON THE READER

When advertisers exert influence over editorial content, readers are deprived of access to critical and impartial information that is necessary to understand local reality. This interference distorts public perception, as published articles tend to favor the interests of those who pay for the ads, rather than the community. Readers receive an incomplete and biased version of the facts, which affects their ability to make informed decisions on relevant issues.

Furthermore, this practice undermines public trust in local journalism, which comes to be seen as an extension of commercial and political interests. The credibility of journalism depends on its independence, and when that independence is compromised, readers become more skeptical and less engaged with the media.

The influence of advertisers on local journalism is a factor that can compromise the impartiality and transparency of information, harming the reader's right to truly independent coverage. By learning to identify signs of advertising influence in articles, you become a more critical reader and able to question the true purpose of the content you consume.

"SPECIAL COVERAGE" AND "SPONSORED PROJECT" - SIGNS OF MANIPULATED CONTENT

In journalism, special coverage and sponsored projects are often presented as public interest reporting that explores a topic in depth, such as a series of stories on health, education, security, or economic development. While these projects can provide relevant information, they are not always produced independently. Companies and public figures often fund these coverages to highlight their actions, promote their brands, and associate their image with topics that appeal to the public.

When presented as "special coverage," these sponsored pieces of content give the impression that they are the result of impartial, investigative work, which can be misleading to the reader. The sponsor—whether a company, a local authority, or a group with specific interests—uses journalism to convey its message in a more subtle way, as the content disguises itself as reporting. In this chapter, we will learn how to identify these sponsored projects and understand the effects they have on public perception.

THE LINE BETWEEN JOURNALISM AND ADVERTISING IN SPECIAL COVERAGES

The fundamental difference between a sponsored project and an independent report is the editorial team's autonomy in choosing the focus and approaches. In an independent special report, the journalist decides what to investigate, with the freedom to explore the different angles of the topic, including criticism and counterpoints. In a sponsored report, the agenda, tone and even the data presented can be influenced by the interests of whoever is financing the content.

Imagine a "special coverage on infrastructure" funded by a large construction company. If the project is sponsored, the newspaper may only cover the advantages of the projects funded by the company, ignoring criticism, environmental problems or labor issues. The reader, without realizing that the content was sponsored, interprets the text as an impartial analysis and may be led to adopt a positive and biased view of the company or the projects it carries out in the city.

HOW TO IDENTIFY SPECIAL COVERAGE AND SPONSORED PROJECTS DISGUISED AS JOURNALISM

1. Check for sponsorship notices

In ethical journalism, sponsored content should be clearly labeled. Look for labels such as "sponsored content," "editorial partnership," or "sponsored by [company name]" at the beginning or end of the content. This helps readers understand that the article has a funded bias and may not reflect a fully independent analysis.

In many cases, however, sponsorship notices are placed discreetly or omitted. When there is no mention of the sponsor and the tone of the text is overly positive, the reader should be suspicious of the impartiality of the coverage.

2. Notice the exclusive focus on a sponsor or a topic favorable to it

Sponsored special coverage tends to focus heavily on the achievements and strengths of a single sponsor or its interests, while omitting critical context. For example, a "special series on the future of education" might be funded by a technology company that provides educational solutions. In this case, the coverage is likely to highlight only the benefits of technology in education, ignoring or minimizing discussions about the limitations and challenges of this model.

If a story consistently features the same sponsor or repeatedly mentions a company's products and services, it's likely promoting a specific agenda. Truly independent stories explore different perspectives and present a more balanced view of the topic.

3. Identify the use of complimentary and promotional language

As with other paid stories, sponsored coverage often uses promotional language to create a positive image. Terms such as "innovative," "transformative," and "model for the future" are common and create an idealized view of the project or public figure in question. These words are rarely accompanied by criticism or analysis of potential risks and challenges, a characteristic of disguised promotional content.

For example, a special series on "urban revitalization projects" sponsored by a construction company might repeatedly extol the positive impact of the projects on the city, without addressing issues of transparency, costs, expropriations, or environmental impacts. The use of laudatory adjectives without deeper analysis indicates that the goal of the coverage is to persuade rather than inform.

4. Notice the absence of counterpoints and multiple sources

Independent coverage often includes a variety of sources and perspectives, giving readers a balanced view of the topic. In sponsored projects, however, it is common for all sources to be affiliated with the sponsor or for only voices that are supportive of the project to be heard. A lack of opinions from independent experts, community members, or critics is a sign that the content may be influenced by the sponsor.

For example, a "special coverage on advances in public health" sponsored by the city government may only mention health managers and municipal authorities, without hearing from patients, health workers or experts who could point out challenges and problems faced by the health system. The lack of plural sources is an indication that the story was created to strengthen the image of the city government, and not to investigate the topic impartially.

5. Observe proximity to strategic events or dates

Publishing special coverage around strategic events, such as inaugurations, election campaigns or product launches, is also a sign of potential sponsorship. Many sponsored projects are scheduled to coincide with important dates, when the public figure or company wants to maximize their visibility and reinforce their positive image with the public.

For example, a "special coverage on sustainable development" published just before the launch of a new green real estate development could indicate that the developer or builder funded the content to associate its image with the concept of sustainability. The proximity to specific events suggests that the content serves a promotional purpose.

PRACTICAL EXERCISE: ANALYZING A "SPECIAL COVERAGE" TO IDENTIFY SPONSORSHIP

To practice analyzing special coverage and identify possible sponsorships, follow this step-by-step guide with an article from your city:

1. **Look for sponsorship notices** : Is there a clear notice that the article is sponsored? Look at the header, footer, and end of the article.
2. **Identify the focus and theme** : Does the coverage focus on a sponsor or present a theme directly favorable to that sponsor?
3. **Assess the language and tone** : Does the article use a lot of positive adjectives and promotional language?
4. **Check for diversity of sources** : Does the coverage include opinions from a variety of sources, or does it only feature voices that support the issue?
5. **Consider the context and publication date** : Does the coverage coincide with an important event or date for the sponsor?

Answering these questions will help you identify whether special coverage was influenced by specific interests and understand how sponsored content impacts your interpretation of the facts.

THE IMPACT OF SPONSORED PROJECTS DISGUISED AS JOURNALISM

Special coverage and sponsored projects, when not clearly indicated, undermine readers' trust in journalism. These stories present a biased and often overly positive version of events, leading the public to believe that the information was independently verified. This creates a manipulated perception and undermines citizens' ability to critically evaluate the actions of local authorities and companies.

Furthermore, by presenting advertising content as reporting, local journalism becomes a propaganda tool, abandoning its role as a critical and independent observer. This practice is especially problematic in small communities, where local media is one of the only sources of information about local events. The lack of transparency makes readers more vulnerable to manipulation and limits their right to access truly impartial information.

Special coverage and sponsored projects have the potential to enrich the debate on important issues, but only when they are presented with transparency. By learning to identify such content and question its impartiality, you become a more critical and aware consumer of information, able to distinguish between investigative journalism and disguised advertising.

AGENDA JOURNALISM - WHEN AGENDA REFLECTS POLITICIANS' INTERESTS

Agenda-driven journalism occurs when media outlets follow agendas defined by the interests of authorities, politicians or specific groups, instead of prioritizing issues that are truly important to the community. This type of coverage creates a distortion in public perception because, by deliberately choosing certain issues and ignoring others, media outlets act as promoters of the agendas of public figures and government agencies.

In local journalism, where newsrooms are smaller and often dependent on close relationships with authorities, agenda-setting journalism is a common practice. Many outlets choose to cover stories that favor local authorities in order to maintain friendly relations and ensure access to privileged information. However, by prioritizing topics that benefit political interests, newspapers neglect topics that are equally or even more relevant to the population, leaving important gaps in the information that reaches the public.

In this chapter, we will understand how agenda-driven journalism manifests itself, how it influences news coverage, and learn to identify when an agenda reflects political interests rather than community needs.

HOW AGENDA-SETTING JOURNALISM IMPACTS NEWS COVERAGE

When a media outlet adopts agenda-driven journalism, it changes its editorial line to align with issues that favor the image and interests of public figures. This can mean excessive coverage of inaugurations, investments and projects by local authorities, while more sensitive issues and problems, such as health, security and lack of infrastructure, are left aside.

This alignment with the political agenda can occur directly, such as when the outlet receives explicit instructions from authorities, or indirectly, when the newspaper decides, on its own, to prioritize topics that it considers politically "safe" in order to avoid conflict. The result is coverage that favors the image of authorities and reinforces the view that they are constantly acting for the benefit of the community, while problematic issues are ignored or minimized.

HOW TO IDENTIFY AGENDA JOURNALISM

1. Observe the frequency of articles about the same topic or public figure

One of the clearest signs of agenda-driven journalism is the constant repetition of articles about the same topic or public figure. When a media outlet continually highlights the actions of an authority figure without addressing related problems, failures or criticisms, this indicates that the newspaper is promoting that figure's agenda.

For example, if a newspaper regularly publishes articles about a mayor's inaugurations, visits and "commitments", while topics such as sanitation, public transport or housing do not receive the same attention, it is likely that the outlet is following an editorial line that favors the mayor's agenda. The lack of diversity in the topics covered impoverishes public debate and limits the population's access to a more complete and critical view of local issues.

2. Identify recurring themes that benefit public authorities

In agenda-driven journalism, it is common for specific topics to be frequently covered, especially those that reinforce a positive image of local authorities. The construction of leisure spaces, educational programs and economic development actions are some examples of topics that frequently appear in such coverage. Although these issues are, in fact, important, their continuous and enthusiastic coverage, without critical analysis or the inclusion of counterpoints, suggests that the journalism is aligned with political interests.

If, when reading local news, you notice that certain topics are constantly addressed, while problems that directly affect the community, such as lack of doctors, quality of education and security, are ignored, there is a good chance that the newspaper is following a political agenda.

3. Be wary of the lack of critical articles on public management

One of the fundamental roles of journalism is to monitor the actions of authorities and question their actions for the benefit of society. However, in agenda-driven journalism, this role is left aside to avoid criticism that could compromise the media outlet's relationship with the public administration.

When a local newspaper only publishes articles that are favorable to the administration and avoids investigative reporting on problematic issues—such as the use of public funds, suspicious contracts, or failure to act in critical areas—it is an indication that it is aligned with the authorities' agenda. If the coverage is always positive and there are no investigations into sensitive issues, the newspaper fails to exercise its oversight role, acting more as a mouthpiece for the administration than as an independent source of information.

4. Analyze the choice of sources and statements

Another sign that a news outlet is pushing a political agenda is the choice of sources. In agenda-driven journalism, the main sources are usually the authorities themselves or people who are part of the administration, while ordinary citizens, independent experts and representatives of the opposition rarely have a voice.

For example, if an article about a new housing policy only contains statements from authorities and does not include the opinions of residents, urban planners or housing rights organizations, this indicates limited coverage that favors the official view. Selective choice of sources reveals bias in the coverage and prevents the reader from having access to different perspectives on the topic.

5. Understand the tone of the published articles

Stories that follow a political agenda often have an optimistic and positive tone, seeking to highlight the achievements of the local authority and minimize or omit the challenges faced. Expressions such as "great achievement", "significant progress" and "commitment to well-being" are common and reflect an attempt to create a favorable narrative for the government.

If you notice that the tone of the articles is almost always enthusiastic and complimentary, and that issues such as failures, criticisms or difficulties are left out, it is likely that the newspaper is aligning itself with the interests of the authorities. This tone of coverage becomes even more suspicious when it is accompanied by the absence of critical information or questions.

PRACTICAL EXERCISE: ANALYZING A STORY TO IDENTIFY AGENDA-SETTING JOURNALISM

To practice analyzing agenda journalism, choose a story about a public figure or a government project and ask the following questions:

1. **Is the topic overly frequently discussed?** See if the topic is frequently covered in the newspaper and if it is always treated in a positive way.
2. **Does the topic favor the image of the authority?** Ask yourself whether the article praises the public figure and omits critical issues.
3. **Are there critical articles about the management?** Try to identify whether the newspaper publishes investigative or critical reports about the authority's performance.
4. **What sources are consulted?** Check whether the main sources are authorities and whether there is an absence of independent experts, residents or members of the opposition.
5. **What is the tone of the article?** Assess whether the tone is enthusiastic and seeks to exalt authority without considering the challenges or potential problems.

These questions help to understand whether the story is part of coverage guided by political interests, promoting a favorable and limited view of the topic.

THE IMPACT OF AGENDA JOURNALISM ON THE POPULATION

Agenda-driven journalism compromises the population's right to access balanced and diverse information. By choosing topics that reinforce the image of authorities and ignoring real problems that affect daily life, the media manipulates public perception, creating a distorted view of reality. This undermines the community's ability to critically evaluate the actions of authorities and demand improvements in areas where local government is failing.

Furthermore, when local journalism adopts a political agenda, it undermines public trust in the press. Instead of being seen as independent and trustworthy sources, newspapers become perceived as propaganda tools for politicians and interest groups. This practice also reduces civic engagement, as the public, when they perceive that the media outlets are aligned with power, may stop seeking information or questioning government actions.

Agenda-driven journalism is a practice that undermines the impartiality and credibility of media outlets, distorting news coverage to benefit authorities and political figures. By learning to identify signs of agenda-driven journalism, you become a more critical and aware reader, able to assess when a story reflects political interests and when it is truly committed to independent information.

EDITING MANEUVERS - PHOTOS, TITLES AND HIGHLIGHTS THAT DIRECT PUBLIC OPINION

In a news story, photos, headlines and highlights are not just details: they are strategic elements that often guide the reader's understanding and opinion on the topic. The power of these choices is enormous, especially in local journalism, where many people form their views on public figures and events based on images and headlines. When these tools are used in a biased way, journalism ceases to be impartial and begins to manipulate public perception to favor or harm a certain figure or action.

In ethical journalism, the use of images, headlines, and highlights should reflect the actual content of the story, without exaggerating qualities or minimizing problems. However, this is not always the case. Local media outlets often choose photos, write headlines, and highlight excerpts that manipulate the tone of the story and direct the reader toward a specific interpretation. In this chapter, we will learn to identify these editing maneuvers and understand how they influence public perception, especially when it comes to local issues.

HOW PHOTOS, TITLES AND HIGHLIGHTS MANIPULATE READER PERCEPTION

The choice of an image, the wording of a title or the emphasis on a sentence directly influence the reader's emotions and reactions. These elements act as "gateways" to the article, setting the tone and establishing a first impression that often persists even after reading the entire content. A photo showing a smiling politician surrounded by supporters conveys an image of closeness and acceptance, while a photo showing him alone or in a tense pose suggests the opposite.

Similarly, a positive headline can convince the reader that the action or project in question is beneficial, while a negative headline can discourage support and create a critical view. Highlights, which are excerpts chosen to draw attention, also play an important role in constructing a narrative and can emphasize specific aspects of the article, leading the reader to focus on those points rather than evaluating the content as a whole.

HOW TO IDENTIFY EDITING MANEUVERS IN PHOTOS, TITLES AND HIGHLIGHTS

1. Observe the use of photos and the context of the images

Photos are powerful tools in creating a visual narrative, and the choice of an image can directly influence the reader's perception of a public figure or an event. In an article about a mayor, for example, a photo of him in a familiar environment or in contact with the public creates a positive and welcoming image. On the other hand, an image that shows him in a tense situation, with a serious expression or isolated in an institutional environment, can suggest coldness, distance or lack of support.

To identify photo manipulation, look at the context of the image: are there people around, showing support? Does the politician or public figure seem approachable and friendly, or distant and unapproachable? Also, compare it with other photos published in different media outlets to see if there is an attempt to manipulate public perception by emphasizing certain angles or expressions.

2. Analyze the tone of the title and the type of language used

Headlines are the first information readers receive about a story, and they play an important role in shaping their expectations and even their judgments about the content. Biased headlines often use loaded adjectives or verbs that can exaggerate the good things about an action or minimize its problems. For example, a headline like "Mayor Brings Big Improvements to Local Health Care" suggests that the action was largely positive, even if the story itself has little concrete evidence of that impact.

Note whether the headline makes statements or judgments that are not supported by the body of the text. Unbiased headlines tend to be direct and descriptive, without adjectives or verbs that indicate emotion. Choosing neutral, objective language is a sign that the headline is designed to inform rather than influence.

3. Identify the highlights and question why they were chosen

Highlights are sentences or excerpts that are highlighted in the edition to draw the reader's attention. These highlights are often used to emphasize the most favorable view or point of view of the article, giving less visibility to critical passages or counterpoints. When reading an article, notice which sentences were highlighted and ask yourself why they were chosen over others.

For example, in an article about a new public policy, a headline that says "This initiative will improve the lives of all residents, says the mayor" emphasizes the positive point of view. A more balanced choice would also include a critical opinion or a question about the impact of the measure. When headlines are used to emphasize complimentary or optimistic statements, the media outlet is directing the reader's perception.

4. Be wary of excessive use of supporting images or visual symbols.

In addition to direct photos of public figures, some articles use visual symbols to influence perception.

In articles about public safety, for example, the use of images of police cars, weapons or people in vulnerable situations can generate a sense of urgency and fear. In articles about progress or development, images of modern buildings or happy people in public places suggest prosperity and well-being.

This visual manipulation creates an emotional atmosphere that can influence the way the reader interprets the story. If a story about public safety investments repeatedly uses images of police cars and armed police officers, the reader may interpret the situation as a crisis, even if the data does not indicate a significant increase in crime. These visual choices influence perception and reinforce the message that the media outlet wants to convey.

5. Analyze the coherence between the title, the photos and the content of the article.

Sometimes, the titles and photos used to introduce an article do not correspond to the actual content, creating an expectation in the reader that is not sustained throughout the text. This type of mismatch is a form of manipulation, as it uses the first impression (title and photo) to influence the reader before they even have access to the complete information.

If the headline of an article about a new public project says "New park transforms community," but the content discusses the construction challenges, high costs, and planning issues, there is an intentional mismatch between the headline and the content. This unfair practice manipulates perception, as many readers focus more on the visual elements and the headline than on the body of the article.

PRACTICAL EXERCISE: ANALYZING PHOTOS, TITLES AND HIGHLIGHTS IN AN ARTICLE

To practice critical analysis of photos, titles and highlights, choose a recent article about a public figure or a project in your city and do the following analysis:

1. **Look at the photo used** : What does the image suggest about the subject or public figure? Are the expression, context and visual elements positive, negative or neutral?
2. **Analyze the title** : Is the title descriptive or biased? Does it use adjectives, exaggerate qualities, or minimize criticisms?
3. **Identify highlights** : Which sentences are highlighted? Do they reinforce a positive or negative view? Are there counterpoints or just favorable statements?
4. **Evaluate the coherence between the elements** : Do the title, photo and highlights correspond to the actual content of the article? Or is there an attempt

to create an impression that does not reflect the reality of the facts?

Answering these questions allows you to recognize editing maneuvers and avoid being influenced by biased visual and editorial choices.

THE IMPACT OF EDITING MANOEUVRES ON PUBLIC PERCEPTION

The choices of photos, headlines and highlights affect the reader's perception in powerful and subtle ways. When these elements are used to manipulate public opinion, they create a favorable or unfavorable narrative that influences the public's understanding without them realizing it. In responsible journalism, these elements are used to enrich the information, offering an objective and fair view. However, in biased journalism, they are used to reinforce partial narratives, promoting or harming public figures according to the interests of the media outlet.

Manipulation through these visual and editorial elements also weakens the credibility of journalism, as the public begins to distrust the intentions and impartiality of media outlets. By learning to identify these maneuvers, you become better prepared to consume information consciously and critically, avoiding forced interpretations.

Photos, headlines and highlights are tools that, when used in a biased way, can direct public opinion and manipulate the reader's perception. By identifying and questioning these elements, you become a more attentive reader and able to perceive the intentions behind the editorial choice, maintaining a critical and balanced view.

DISCREET COVERAGE OF LOCAL CRISES AND SCANDALS

In small and medium-sized cities, where the relationship between journalists, authorities and businesspeople tends to be closer, coverage of local crises and scandals is often handled discreetly or even silenced. This practice, known as "discreet coverage", occurs when media outlets choose to reduce or omit the visibility of serious problems, avoiding investigating or highlighting issues that could harm public figures or influential institutions.

This lack of transparency undermines journalism's role as a watchdog of power and prevents the public from having access to complete and relevant information. By downplaying scandals or crises, the local press protects specific interests, creating a narrative that favors the authorities and weakens citizens' right to demand transparency and accountability.

In this chapter, we'll explore how to spot signs of undercover coverage, understand the motivations behind this practice, and learn how to seek alternative information when local journalism fails to report on important issues.

WHY DOES THE PRESS AVOID LOCAL SCANDALS?

There are several reasons why local journalism chooses not to highlight crises and scandals. Some of the main ones include:

- **Financial dependence** : Many local newspapers depend on advertising and sponsorship from city halls, council members or companies linked to government. Covering scandals involving these figures can put this source of income at risk.
- **Personal relationships** : In smaller communities, journalists, politicians and businesspeople often share social and professional circles, making critical and independent coverage difficult.
- **Privileged access** : Maintaining good relations with public figures is a strategy to ensure exclusivity in information and interviews. Criticizing these authorities can result in restricted access to important data.
- **Fear of retaliation** : In some regions, reporting scandals can lead to legal retaliation or even personal threats against journalists and media outlets.

The result is local journalism that prioritizes maintaining friendly relations with those in power instead of informing the population about relevant and, often, serious issues.

HOW TO IDENTIFY DISCREET COVERAGE OF CRISES AND SCANDALS

1. Notice the lack of news on controversial topics

One of the clearest signs that a crisis is being treated discreetly or ignored by the local press is the lack of coverage of the issue. Even when a serious issue is widely discussed on social media or in mainstream media outlets, local newspapers may choose not to cover it or only mention it superficially.

For example, if there is a scandal involving misappropriation of public funds in the city hall and the local newspaper does not publish any investigative reports, limiting itself to republishing official notes or versions provided by those involved, this indicates a deliberate choice to minimize the issue.

2. Analyze the tone and depth of coverage

Even when crises are reported, the tone and depth of the story can reveal an attempt to soften the impact. News stories that cover controversial topics vaguely, without detailing the facts, or that present only official statements, without investigating the details, suggest discreet coverage.

For example, an article that reports a complaint against a local authority, but uses expressions such as "alleged problem" or "possible irregularity", and that does not provide information about ongoing investigations or expert testimonies, is trying to minimize the seriousness of the case.

3. Check for lack of continuity in the reports

Discreet coverage often includes only one or two articles on the topic, published briefly and without continuity. This strategy reduces the visibility of the crisis and prevents the public from following its developments.

If a corruption allegation, for example, is reported only once, with no updates on investigations or court hearings, it is likely that the newspaper chose to end coverage quickly to avoid conflict with the parties involved.

4. Identify focus on alternative themes

Another common strategy is to divert the public's attention to other issues. During a crisis, the local press may choose to prioritize positive news or irrelevant events, creating a "smokescreen" to divert the focus away from the problems.

For example, if a councilor is involved in a scandal and, in the same period, the newspaper publishes repeated articles about small inaugurations or cultural events, this may be an attempt to redirect public interest.

5. Compare local coverage with other carriers

When local media choose to downplay a crisis, other outlets, such as state or national news outlets, may cover the issue in more depth. Comparing local coverage with that of other sources is an effective way to identify gaps and omissions.

If a scandal involving the city hall is highlighted in larger newspapers but is given superficial or absent treatment in local media, it is likely that the city's press is trying to protect the officials involved.

PRACTICAL EXERCISE: INVESTIGATING CRISES AND SCANDALS IN LOCAL MEDIA

Choose a recent controversial topic in your city, such as complaints against public figures or problems with essential services, and do the following analysis:

1. **Look for news on the topic in local newspapers** : Was the topic covered? Was the coverage detailed or superficial?
2. **Compare with other media outlets** : Are regional or national newspapers covering the topic? Is their coverage more in-depth than that of local newspapers?
3. **Observe the continuity of coverage** : Have there been updates or was the story published just once?
4. **Analyze the presence of alternative topics** : Did the local newspaper prioritize other topics during the crisis period? Do these topics divert attention from the problem?

5. **Check the tone of the articles** : Does the text downplay the seriousness of the topic? Does it use vague or overly cautious language?

Answering these questions will help you identify whether the crisis is being handled discreetly and seek alternative sources for more complete information.

HOW TO SEARCH FOR INFORMATION WHEN LOCAL PRESS FAILS

If you feel that local coverage is omitting or watering down a relevant topic, there are other ways to get informed:

- **Social media and community groups** : Many complaints and debates begin on social media and local forums. While these sources need to be verified, they can provide preliminary information on the topic.
- **Regional or national newspapers** : Larger-reach outlets can cover local crises with more independence and depth.
- **Transparency portals and public documents** : In cases of complaints related to public contracts or budgets, transparency portals and access to information requests can provide important data.
- **Independent media organizations** : Independent blogs and portals often have fewer financial ties to local authorities and can address issues that are ignored by mainstream media.

THE IMPACT OF SILENCE ON LOCAL CRISES

When local journalism chooses to minimize or ignore crises and scandals, it weakens oversight of power and undermines transparency in public management. This silence allows problems to be swept under the rug, leaving the population uninformed and unable to hold authorities accountable.

Furthermore, the practice of discreet coverage reduces public trust in the local press, which is then seen as colluding with the interests of the authorities. This weakens the role of journalism as a pillar of democracy and contributes to the perpetuation of opaque political practices.

Covering crises and scandals discreetly undermines transparency and undermines public trust in local journalism. By learning to spot the signs of this practice and seeking out alternative sources of information, you can protect yourself from manipulation and ensure that you are well-informed about the issues that really matter in your city.

SILENT OPPOSITION - WHY LOCAL JOURNALISM IGNORES CERTAIN GROUPS

In journalism, giving space to different voices and points of view is essential to ensure balanced and democratic coverage. However, in many cities, local media outlets choose to ignore or downplay opposition voices, silencing groups critical of the authorities and creating a unified narrative that favors the government. This silence on opposition groups is not just an omission; it is a strategy that shapes public perception, reinforces the power of government figures, and marginalizes those who question or denounce controversial practices.

When critical voices are silenced, public debate becomes one-sided, and the public loses the opportunity to hear different perspectives on important issues. This practice undermines journalism's role as an impartial mediator and instead turns local media into an extension of the public relations department of the authorities. In this chapter, we will explore why local journalism ignores opposition groups, the effects of this omission, and how to identify and seek out alternative sources that bring critical voices back into the public debate.

WHY ARE CERTAIN CRITICAL GROUPS IGNORED BY LOCAL MEDIA?

There are several reasons why local journalism avoids giving space to opposition groups or critical voices:

- **Financial dependence**: Media outlets that receive financial support from city halls, councilors or large companies often avoid publishing articles that directly criticize these funders, for fear of losing sponsorship or advertising.
- **Social and political proximity**: In small towns, journalists, politicians and businesspeople often share social circles and interests. This creates a resistance to giving space to critical voices, which can destabilize these relationships.
- **Interest in maintaining privileged access**: Covering the opposition or giving visibility to criticism may result in losing access to privileged information from government figures or local authorities.
- **Fear of reprisals**: In some regions, journalists who highlight opposition groups face threats, lawsuits or even physical violence, leading them to avoid conflict.

These dynamics create an environment where the local press becomes increasingly dependent and aligned with the interests of the current power, abandoning the mission of guaranteeing plurality and transparency in information.

HOW EXCLUSION OF OPPOSITION SHAPES THE LOCAL NARRATIVE

The absence of critical voices in local news has profound effects on public perception. Without hearing from the opposition, the community is exposed only to the official view, which creates a false sense of consensus and reduces the space for questioning. Furthermore, ignoring critical groups allows local governments and powerful companies to escape increased scrutiny, perpetuating questionable practices without facing significant resistance.

For example, if a local newspaper covers a new housing policy promoted by the city government but does not give space to groups that point out flaws in the project or to residents who say they have been harmed, the public will only have access to the official narrative, which is likely to emphasize the benefits of the project and ignore its problems. This type of coverage creates a one-sided perception and prevents society from seeing the full picture of the situation.

HOW TO IDENTIFY SILENCE ABOUT OPPOSITION GROUPS

1. Note the lack of counterpoints in articles on public policies

Stories that cover public policies in a one-sided manner, without including criticism or counterpoints, are a clear sign that local media is ignoring opposition voices. For example, if a story about the city budget only features statements from the mayor or the finance team, without hearing from opposition council members or independent experts, this indicates that the story is aligned with the official narrative.

In ethical journalism, it is common to hear multiple sides of an issue. The lack of counterpoints, especially on controversial topics, is an indication that local media is avoiding giving space to critical voices.

2. Check for coverage of protests or critical demonstrations

Another sign that local journalism ignores the opposition is the lack of coverage of protests, demonstrations or actions critical of the government. Even when these events attract large audiences or address relevant issues, they may be ignored or treated superficially by the media.

If the population mobilizes against a government decision — such as a tariff increase or budget cuts — and the local newspaper does not cover the event, or only mentions official figures or statements, it is likely that the outlet is trying to reduce the visibility of the opposition.

3. Analyze whether the opposition is mentioned only in a negative way

When the opposition is ignored by the local media, it often only appears in stories that portray it in a negative light. In this case, the media choose to highlight internal conflicts, disagreements or unpopular attitudes of critical groups, reinforcing an unfavorable image.

For example, an article that mentions opposition councilors may focus on criticizing their performance or pointing out differences within the group, without making statements or explaining their proposals. This biased approach reduces the credibility of the opposition and reinforces the narrative that it is not relevant or effective.

4. Note the absence of critical figures in the interviews and analyses

Another way to identify silence about the opposition is to check whether critical or independent figures appear as sources in articles that analyze public policies or issues relevant to the city. If only government officials and allies are interviewed, the reader has access to a limited and biased view of the facts.

For example, in a report on problems with public transport, the absence of statements from unions, civil organizations or opposition representatives suggests that the newspaper is avoiding including criticism of the government or the companies responsible for the service.

5. Compare local coverage with discussions on social media or other outlets

Social media and independent outlets often highlight complaints or criticisms that don't appear in traditional media. Comparing local news with online discussions can reveal gaps in coverage and show which voices are being ignored.

For example, if community groups or local influencers mention irregularities in a public project, but the newspaper does not cover the topic or does so only superficially, this indicates that the media is avoiding giving visibility to these criticisms.

PRACTICAL EXERCISE: IDENTIFYING SILENCE ABOUT OPPOSITION

To better understand how local journalism deals with critical groups, choose a public policy or relevant topic in your city and analyze:

1. **Which sources are consulted?** Does the article present statements from opponents or only from authorities and allies?
2. **Were protests or criticism addressed?** Did the newspaper cover demonstrations or critical actions on the topic? If so, was the focus positive, neutral or negative?
3. **Compare with social media or alternative outlets** : Are there criticisms or relevant information being discussed outside of traditional journalism?

4. **Does the tone of the article favor the official view?**
   Does the text reinforce the government's narrative without presenting significant counterpoints?

This exercise helps you identify whether local media is silencing critical groups and seek more complete and balanced information from other sources.

THE IMPACT OF SILENCE ON CRITICAL GROUPS

Ignoring opposition in local journalism weakens democratic debate and undermines oversight of government. Without access to different perspectives, the public loses the opportunity to question policies and demand improvements. Furthermore, silence on critical voices reinforces the perception that authorities are always acting correctly, even when there are flaws or irregularities to be pointed out.

By marginalizing opposition groups, local media also reinforce political inequalities, making it harder for independent voices to be heard and for alternative proposals to be considered. This creates an environment of conformity and reduces public pressure on governments, weakening mechanisms of social control.

Silence about opposition groups is a strategy that undermines plurality and transparency in local journalism. By learning to recognize this practice, you can seek out alternative sources and ensure that you are accessing a broader and more balanced view of the facts.

DIFFERENT SOURCES AND CONTRASTING OPINIONS - HOW TO IDENTIFY A WELL-RECORDED STORY

One of the cornerstones of quality, ethical journalism is the use of multiple sources to ensure that coverage of a topic is comprehensive, balanced, and impartial. By listening to multiple voices—including authorities, experts, affected citizens, and critics—journalists provide the public with a broad, contextualized view of the facts, allowing readers to form their own opinions based on complete and reliable information.

However, in local journalism, it is common to find stories that use only one source or that prioritize voices aligned with the interests of authorities or influential companies. This results in partial and limited coverage that does not reflect the complexity of the topics covered. In this chapter, we will explore how to identify a well-researched story, recognize the importance of diverse sources, and understand how opposing opinions contribute to more balanced journalism.

WHAT DEFINES A WELL-RECOVERED SUBJECT?

A well-researched subject is one that:

- Includes multiple sources, representing different sides of an issue.
- It offers historical and social context so that the reader understands the relevance of the topic.

- Brings contradictory opinions to balance the narrative and avoid bias.
- Presents concrete data and verified information to support the claims made.
- It reflects an effort by the journalist to investigate, question and go beyond official statements.

When these characteristics are present, journalism fulfills its function of providing in-depth information and promoting a healthy and democratic public debate.

WHY ARE DIVERSE SOURCES ESSENTIAL IN JOURNALISM?

By including multiple sources, journalists ensure that their story represents a variety of perspectives and avoids bias. Each source brings a unique contribution, whether technical, emotional or critical, and together they help to build a richer, more balanced narrative.

For example, when covering a housing project, a well-researched story should include:

- **Authorities** : To explain the project, its objectives and the investments involved.
- **Affected residents** : To report how the initiative directly impacts the community.
- **Independent experts** : To assess technical merits and point out possible flaws.
- **Critical or opposition groups** : To raise questions or concerns about the project.

Without these diverse voices, coverage is incomplete and may lead readers to believe there is consensus on the topic, when in fact there are debates and controversies to be considered.

HOW TO IDENTIFY ARTICLES THAT INCLUDE MULTIPLE SOURCES

1. Check the number of sources cited

A well-researched article usually cites multiple sources, representing different sides of an issue. If your article only includes statements from authorities or a single source, it is likely not to provide a balanced view of the issue.

For example, a story about changes to public transport should include testimonials from users, mobility experts, representatives of the companies responsible for the service, and local authorities. If only statements from authorities appear, the coverage is incomplete.

2. Check if there is diversity of profiles among the sources

In addition to the number of sources, the diversity of profiles is equally important. An article that only features authorities and academic experts, for example, may ignore the practical impact of a decision on the population. Likewise, articles that prioritize only ordinary citizens may lack a technical analysis of the topic.

Look for articles that combine different types of sources, such as:

- Government representatives.
- Technical and academic experts.
- Civil society organizations.
- Directly affected groups (residents, workers, service users).
- Critics and members of the opposition.

This diversity helps to build a more complete and detailed view of the topic.

3. Analyze whether there are contradictory opinions or counterpoints

An essential characteristic of a well-researched article is the inclusion of contradictory opinions. When an issue is controversial or contentious, it is important that the article presents the different sides of the debate, giving the reader the opportunity to evaluate the arguments and form their own opinion.

For example, in an article about the construction of a power plant, it is important that the following appear:

- Authorities who defend the project as an economic advance.
- Environmentalists who point out possible environmental impacts.
- Experts who evaluate the technical and financial aspects of the work.
- Residents of the region who may be impacted positively or negatively.

If a story does not include counterpoints and simply repeats the official view, it fails to provide a balanced overview.

4. Assess the depth and context presented

Well-researched articles not only report the facts, but also contextualize them. They explain why the topic is important, what its implications are, and how it relates to larger issues. They also include concrete, historical data that helps the reader understand the complexity of the topic.

For example, an article about tax increases might include information such as:

- What is the city's revenue collection history?
- How the new taxes will be applied and who will be most impacted.
- Comparisons with other cities of similar size.
- Opinions of economists and statements by small business owners and workers.

Without this context, coverage becomes superficial and may not accurately reflect reality.

HOW TO RECOGNIZE STORIES THAT LACK MULTIPLE SOURCES

1. Lack of plurality in statements

When a story presents only one side of the story or cites only one source, it is limited and biased. For example, if a story about public safety cites only the mayor and the police, ignoring experts, citizens, and human rights organizations, it is omitting important voices.

2. Exclusive focus on official statements

Articles that limit themselves to reproducing notes or statements from public bodies without questioning or investigating them are not offering quality journalistic coverage.

3. Lack of data and analysis

An article that does not present numbers, statistics or expert analysis lacks foundation. Without concrete data, the reader does not have the necessary tools to critically assess the situation.

4. Ignoring those directly affected by the issue

If the article addresses a public policy or project, but does not include the voice of those who will be directly impacted, it fails to represent the complete reality.

PRACTICAL EXERCISE: ASSESSING THE QUALITY OF A SUBJECT

Choose a recent article published in a local newspaper and answer the following questions:

1. **How many sources were cited?**
2. **Do the sources represent different sides of the issue?**
3. **Are there contradictory opinions or counterpoints?**
4. **Does the article include concrete data and analysis?**
5. **Who was heard: authorities, experts, citizens, critics?**

If the article has few sources, no contradictions, or lacks context, it probably wasn't researched well.

THE IMPACT OF WELL-RESEARCHED MATERIALS ON SOCIETY

When local journalism invests in well-researched stories, it fulfills its role of informing the population in an ethical and comprehensive manner. By offering different perspectives and opposing opinions, media outlets promote healthy public debate, encourage critical thinking and strengthen democracy.

Furthermore, well-researched articles help combat misinformation and give readers the tools they need to independently evaluate public policies, projects and actions. In communities where access to information is limited, quality journalism is a powerful tool for ensuring transparency and accountability.

Diverse sources and opposing opinions are essential elements of ethical and reliable journalism. By learning to identify well-researched stories, you become a more critical and aware reader, capable of recognizing and valuing journalism that truly contributes to the development of society.

EDITORIAL INDEPENDENCE - WHEN A NEWSPAPER OR BLOG REALLY TELLS THE TRUTH

Editorial independence is the ability of a media outlet to operate without external interference that influences the content published. Whether from advertisers, politicians, businesspeople or other interest groups, independence is essential to ensure that journalism fulfills its main mission: to inform in an impartial, ethical manner that is focused on the public interest.

However, achieving editorial independence in local journalism is particularly challenging. Smaller outlets often rely on local funders to stay afloat, creating an environment where the line between journalism and propaganda can be blurred. In many cases, newspapers and blogs become complicit in the interests of their financial backers, abandoning impartial investigation and prioritizing narratives that favor public figures or advertisers.

This chapter explores how to recognize independent news outlets, the signs of bias, and ways to support honest, ethical journalism in your community.

WHAT DEFINES AN EDITORIALLY INDEPENDENT NEWSPAPER?

An independent media outlet is one that:

1. **It does not depend exclusively on financiers with political or commercial interests.**
2. **Maintains transparency about its funding sources.**
3. **Investigates and publishes information even if it is contrary to the interests of its sponsors or allies.**
4. **Includes multiple sources and diverse opinions in its reporting.**
5. **Prioritizes the public interest above any specific agenda.**

Editorial independence does not mean that a newspaper or blog is completely free from funders or partners, but rather that these supports do not influence the published content.

SIGNS THAT A COMMUNICATION VEHICLE IS INDEPENDENT

1. Transparency on funding

Independent media outlets are generally clear about who their funders are and how they ensure their sustainability. This could include subscriptions, reader donations, well-defined commercial partnerships, or even projects funded by organizations committed to ethical journalism.

If a media outlet is transparent about its sources of income and explains how it maintains its independence, that's a good sign. On the other hand, a lack of information about financing could indicate that the media outlet has hidden ties that could compromise its impartiality.

2. Critical coverage of sensitive topics

An independent newspaper or blog does not hesitate to address sensitive issues, even if this means criticizing influential figures or powerful institutions. Independent media outlets have the courage to question public decisions, investigate irregularities and give visibility to complaints, even when this may generate conflict.

If you notice that an outlet fearlessly covers allegations against local political figures, reports on corporate scandals, or investigates controversial topics, it indicates that it operates with a significant degree of independence.

3. Diversity of voices and perspectives

Editorial independence is reflected in the plurality of sources and opinions included in the articles. Independent media outlets seek to represent different sides of a story, including authorities, experts, ordinary citizens and critical groups.

If a news outlet consistently presents only the official view or a single perspective, it is likely aligned with specific interests. Truly independent journalism, on the other hand, listens to all sides and allows the reader to form their own opinion.

4. Reputation for impartiality over time

Editorial independence is built on consistency. A media outlet that takes an impartial stance on a variety of issues over time demonstrates its commitment to journalistic ethics. Research the media outlet's track record: has it ever taken on influential figures? Does it publish critical stories about different parties or groups? This helps you assess whether it truly acts independently.

5. Clear distinction between opinion and news

Independent media outlets maintain a clear separation between news reports and opinion pieces. This means that when reading a news story, the reader can trust that the content reflects the facts and not the personal opinions of the editors or writers.

If the outlet mixes opinions with facts without making this clear to the reader, this may indicate a lack of commitment to impartiality.

SIGNS THAT A VEHICLE IS NOT INDEPENDENT

1. Too much content that favors sponsors or allies

If a newspaper or blog repeatedly publishes articles that praise a sponsor or public figure without offering criticism or counterpoints, its independence is likely to be compromised.
For example, a media outlet that consistently covers a city hall's actions with a positive tone, but ignores protests or complaints against the administration, is probably aligned with the interests of the local government.

2. Omission of controversial topics

When a media outlet avoids covering crises, scandals or important criticisms, this may be an indication that it is protecting influential figures or avoiding conflicts with funders.

For example, if a local company faces environmental complaints and the newspaper does not publish any articles on the subject, this suggests that the outlet prioritizes preserving its relationship with the company over the public interest.

3. Dependence on ads from a single funder

If a news organization's revenue comes mostly from a single sponsor—such as a city, a large corporation, or a politician—its independence is at risk. This type of financial relationship creates a conflict of interest, where the news organization may be hesitant to publish something that would harm its primary funder.

4. Excessive use of official releases

Media outlets that publish press releases from companies or government agencies as if they were news reports demonstrate a lack of commitment to independent investigation. This behavior generally reflects a relationship of dependence or alignment with the interests of those who provide the press releases.

HOW TO SUPPORT INDEPENDENT VEHICLES

Editorial independence depends not only on the ethical commitment of media outlets, but also on the support of readers and organizations that value impartial journalism. Here are some ways to strengthen and support independent outlets:

1. **Subscribe and contribute financially** : Many independent outlets rely on subscriptions or donations to keep them running. Financially supporting ethical journalism is one way to ensure it continues to exist.
2. **Share quality content** : Help expand the reach of independent media outlets by sharing well-researched and relevant articles on your social networks and contact circles.

3. **Question and value transparency** : Support media outlets that make it clear who their funders are and how they ensure their independence. This encourages ethical and responsible practices.
4. **Consume critically** : Read different media outlets, compare approaches and value those that include multiple sources and opinions.
5. **Report lack of independence** : If you identify media outlets that clearly favor political or economic interests, question their conduct and seek more reliable alternatives.

THE IMPACT OF INDEPENDENT JOURNALISM ON SOCIETY

Editorially independent media outlets play a crucial role in promoting transparency and accountability, especially in smaller communities. They ensure that different perspectives are heard, investigate issues of public interest, and hold power to account, contributing to a more informed and democratic society.

Additionally, independent journalism helps combat misinformation by offering a reliable alternative in a landscape where biased or manipulated news is increasingly common. When you support independent media, you are strengthening democracy and helping to create a society where truth and ethics prevail.

Editorial independence is the foundation of ethical and trustworthy journalism. By learning to recognize independent media outlets and supporting their work, you contribute to a fairer and more transparent information environment, where truth and the public interest prevail over political and commercial agendas.

CRITICAL QUESTIONS TO ASK WHEN READING A STORY

In a world where access to information is abundant but not always reliable, the ability to question journalistic content is essential to staying well informed. Reading a story passively can lead to accepting partial, manipulated or incomplete information, especially in local journalism, where the proximity between media outlets and public figures often results in biased coverage.

Asking critical questions when reading news is a way to develop an active and conscious reading style, assessing whether the content is impartial, well-researched and relevant. In this chapter, we will present a series of questions that you can ask yourself when consuming news, helping you identify biases, gaps and possible hidden intentions behind the articles.

THE CRITICAL QUESTIONS EVERY READER SHOULD ASK

1. Who is the main source of the material?

The first question to ask when reading a news story is: **where does the information come from?** A reliable story usually draws on a variety of well-identified sources, including experts, witnesses, and documents. If the story cites only one source—especially an authority or official body—this may indicate a lack of investigation or alignment with specific interests.

Example: In an article about the launch of a new public policy, ask whether the article includes:

- Statements by authorities defending the policy.
- Opinions from independent experts.
- Reports from citizens who will be affected by the measure.

If the article is limited to reproducing the official view, without seeking counterpoints, it is incomplete.

2. Is the information based on concrete data or opinions?

A good article presents data and evidence to support the claims it makes. Ask yourself: Does **the article include numbers, statistics, or documents that support the information? Or is it based solely on statements and opinions?**

Example: A news story about a reduction in crime should include clear data, such as crime rates recorded before and after the measure. If the story simply says "the city is safer, according to the mayor", without providing any numbers or verifiable sources, it lacks depth and may be propagating propaganda.

3. Which voices are missing?

Another fundamental question is: **who is being ignored in the story?** The silence about certain voices can be as revealing as the information presented.

Example: In a news story about the impact of a large real estate development, check that the text includes:

- The vision of the responsible company.
- Statements from local residents.
- Opinions of independent environmentalists or urban planners.

If the article only presents a positive view of the company, ignoring possible criticism or concerns from the community, it is omitting important information.

4. Does the title reflect the content of the article?

Headlines are often used to capture the reader's attention, but they don't always accurately reflect the content of the text. Ask yourself: **Does the headline match what is being presented, or does it exaggerate and distort the facts?**

Example: A headline like "New project transforms the city" can be misleading if the article only mentions the beginning of a project without detailing the real impacts. Compare the headline with the content and assess whether it is creating an exaggerated narrative.

5. Does the article include opposing opinions?

Ask: **Does the article present different points of view on the topic? Or does it simply reinforce a single perspective?** Well-researched news stories include contradictory opinions, allowing the reader to evaluate the arguments from all sides.

Example: In a news story about a municipal tax increase, the text should include:

- Statements from the city hall explaining the measure.
- Economists' views on financial impacts.
- Reactions from affected businesspeople or citizens.

The absence of counterpoints indicates that the article may be favoring a specific view.

6. Are there hidden interests behind the matter?

Ask yourself: **who benefits from this news?** Some texts may seem impartial at first glance, but in practice they serve to promote a public figure, a company or a specific initiative.

Example: If a story about the success of an environmental policy repeatedly mentions a company sponsoring the project, this could indicate that the content was influenced by commercial interests. Be aware of exaggerated or complimentary mentions, which could indicate hidden sponsorship.

7. Is the tone of the text neutral or emotional?

A well-written article has a neutral, informative tone, while biased texts tend to appeal to emotion or judgment. Ask yourself: Does **the text use opinionated words , such as "great achievement," "disgraceful failure," or "historical transformation"**?

Example: In a news story about a public project, words like "exemplary initiative" suggest a positive bias. A neutral text would simply describe the project, its goals and possible challenges.

8. Does the newspaper or blog indicate the source of the information?

Always ask yourself: **Is the information original or did it come from another source? Is the source reliable?** Ethical media outlets identify the origin of data and statements, such as official reports, academic research or direct interviews.

Example: If an article states that "a recent study shows progress in local education," it should cite the name of the study, the institution responsible for it, and the main results. The absence of these details is a sign of a lack of transparency.

9. Does the article provide historical or comparative context?

Ask yourself: **Does the text explain the history of the topic or make relevant comparisons?**
Comprehensive news stories help the reader understand the evolution of a problem or compare current data with previous periods.
Example: In a news story about a drop in unemployment, the text should include:

- Data from previous years to contextualize the improvement.
- Comparisons with other cities or states.
- External factors that may have influenced the numbers.

Without context, news can be manipulated to appear more positive or negative than it really is.

10. Are there any indications that the article may be sponsored?

Finally, ask: **Are there any signs that the story was influenced by sponsors?** These include:

- Repetitive mentions of a company or public figure.
- Absence of criticism or counterpoints.
- Use of promotional or emotional language.

If a story appears to favor a group or person without questioning them, it may be sponsored or biased.

PRACTICAL EXERCISE: APPLYING CRITICAL QUESTIONS TO A SUBJECT

Choose a news story published in a local newspaper and analyze it based on the questions above. Answer:

1. Who are the sources cited? Is there diversity?
2. Does the article include concrete data or is it based solely on statements?
3. Which voices are missing?
4. Does the title reflect the content of the text?
5. Are there any conflicting opinions?
6. Who can benefit from this news?
7. Is the tone of the text neutral or emotional?
8. Is the origin of the information indicated?
9. Does the article provide historical or comparative context?
10. Are there signs of sponsorship or outside influence?

This exercise helps you identify strengths and weaknesses in news coverage, making you a more critical and aware consumer of information.

Asking critical questions when reading an article is a way to exercise your role as a conscious and well-informed citizen. By adopting this practice, you not only avoid being manipulated by partial information, but you also become able to evaluate the quality of the journalism you consume, strengthening your understanding of the issues that impact your life and your community.

UNDERSTAND THE ROLE OF MAYORS AND COUNCILORS - THEIR FUNCTIONS AND RESPONSIBILITIES

Mayors and city council members play fundamental roles in municipal management, but the public is often unaware of their roles and responsibilities. This lack of knowledge can lead to inappropriate demands or the acceptance of questionable practices, as it is not always clear what these public figures can or cannot do within their responsibilities.

Understanding the roles of mayors and city council members is essential to assessing whether they are fulfilling their obligations and to making more informed and effective demands. Furthermore, knowing their limits of action helps prevent exaggerated campaign promises or manipulative political speeches from distorting public perception of what can actually be done.

In this chapter, we will explore the roles and responsibilities of mayors and council members, highlighting the limits of their actions and how these figures can directly impact their community.

THE ROLE OF THE MAYOR IN MUNICIPAL ADMINISTRATION

The mayor is the head of the municipal executive branch, responsible for managing the city's resources and public services. His or her main function is to implement public policies that meet the needs of the population, ensuring the proper functioning of essential areas such as health, education, transportation and infrastructure.

MAIN RESPONSIBILITIES OF THE MAYOR

1. **Preparing and executing the municipal budget**
   The mayor is responsible for planning how the municipality's resources will be collected and spent. He or she must submit the Budget Bill to the City Council annually, where it will be discussed and approved by the council members.
2. **Manage public services**
   The mayor directly or through departments manages services such as garbage collection, public transportation, municipal health, schools, street and park maintenance, among others.
3. **Develop and implement public policies**
   It must create programs and actions that improve the population's quality of life, such as housing projects, preventive health programs, investments in urban mobility and cultural initiatives.
4. **Comply with and enforce municipal laws**
   The mayor must ensure that laws passed by the City Council are applied and respected.
5. **Representing the municipality**
   In negotiations and partnerships with state and federal governments and private entities, the mayor acts as the official representative of the municipality. He seeks external resources, such as state and federal transfers, to finance local projects.

6. **Appointing municipal secretaries**
   The mayor chooses the secretaries who will lead the different areas of the administration, such as health, education and security. These secretaries are directly responsible for implementing the policies of each sector.

LIMITS ON THE MAYOR'S ACTION

Although the mayor has broad powers at the municipal level, he faces important limitations:

- **Federal and state laws** : The mayor cannot create laws that conflict with state or federal law. For example, he cannot change the Penal Code or create taxes that are not provided for in the Constitution.
- **Budget control** : Municipal revenue is limited and often depends on state and federal transfers. This restricts the resources available for investment.
- **Oversight of councilors** : The mayor's actions are supervised by the City Council, which can call him to account and approve or reject his projects.

THE ROLE OF COUNCILORS IN THE CITY COUNCIL

Council members are representatives of the municipal legislative branch, elected to oversee the mayor, draft laws and act as the voice of the population in the City Council. They are essential to ensuring that public administration is transparent, ethical and aligned with the interests of citizens.

MAIN RESPONSIBILITIES OF COUNCILORS

1. **Draft and approve municipal laws**
   Councilors create laws that regulate various aspects of life in the municipality, such as urban zoning, local traffic, environmental preservation, health and education.
2. **Overseeing the Executive Branch**
   One of the most important functions of city council members is to oversee the actions of the mayor, ensuring that the budget is executed correctly and that public policies are effective. This includes:
   - Require detailed reports on the application of resources.
   - Investigate reports of irregularities.
   - Approve or reject the municipality's accounts.
3. **Approve the municipal budget**
   The mayor cannot spend public funds without the approval of the budget by the City Council. The councilors analyze and discuss the proposal sent by the Executive Branch, and may suggest amendments to change the allocation of funds.
4. **Act as intermediaries between the population and the government**
   Councilors have the role of listening to the community's demands and forwarding them to the mayor or the responsible departments.

5. **Proposing motions and requests for information**
   In addition to creating laws, councilors can propose motions of repudiation, requests for information from the Executive and requests to investigate or demand explanations from local authorities.

LIMITS ON THE ACTION OF COUNCILORS

City council members do not have the power to execute public works or create government programs. Their role is limited to drafting laws, monitoring the executive branch, and representing the community. Campaign promises involving the construction of schools, hospitals, or paving of streets are often unrealistic, since these are the responsibility of the mayor, not the city council members.

HOW MAYORS AND COUNCILORS IMPACT THEIR COMMUNITY

Mayors and city council members have a direct impact on the lives of citizens. Their decisions affect everything from everyday issues, such as street cleaning and public transportation, to long-term issues, such as investment in education and urban development.

PRACTICAL EXAMPLES OF IMPACT:

- **Mayors** :
    - They decide where new schools and hospitals will be built.

- They can implement social assistance and poverty alleviation programs.
- They define priorities for infrastructure works, such as paving streets and basic sanitation.
- **Councilors:**
  - They can create laws that regulate local commerce, encouraging small businesses.
  - They monitor contracts signed by the city government, ensuring that resources are used properly.
  - They act as spokespersons for the population, reporting problems and pressuring the Executive for solutions.

HOW TO EVALUATE THE PERFORMANCE OF MAYORS AND COUNCILORS

1. Track your actions

- Mayors: Check whether the government plan presented during the campaign is being fulfilled. Analyze how the city's resources are being used and which projects have been implemented.
- Councilors: Look at how many bills they have proposed and whether they are actively monitoring the Executive.

2. Consult transparency portals

Access transparency portals to check how the municipal budget is being spent and whether there are irregularities.

3. Compare promises with accomplishments

Assess whether the promises made during the campaign were fulfilled or whether they were unfeasible.

4. Participate in public hearings

Mayors and city council members often hold hearings to discuss public policies. Participating in these events is a way to closely monitor their actions and demand direct responses.

5. Observe transparency and ethics

Mayors and city council members must act transparently and be accountable for their actions. Any sign of unethical conduct or misappropriation of funds is a warning sign to question their actions.

Knowing the roles and responsibilities of mayors and council members is the first step towards exercising active and conscious citizenship. These figures have a direct impact on their communities, but they are also subject to limitations that must be understood so that demands are realistic and effective.

CITIZEN RIGHTS - HOW AND WHERE TO QUESTION REPRESENTATIVES

Every citizen has the right to question and demand action from their elected representatives. This is one of the fundamental pillars of democracy. Mayors and city council members, as local managers and legislators, have the obligation to account for their decisions and explain how they are using public resources to benefit the community.

However, many citizens do not know how to exercise this right or have doubts about what tools are available to question their representatives. The good news is that there are several channels and strategies that can be used to demand greater transparency and participation in public management. In this chapter, we will explore these tools and understand how to use them effectively to demand answers and changes.

WHY IS QUESTIONING ESSENTIAL?

Holding your representatives accountable is more than a right; it is a civic duty. When the population demands transparency and accountability, government officials are more attentive to the community's demands and less likely to act negligently or dishonestly. Furthermore, constant questioning strengthens the relationship between citizens and government, ensuring that decisions are made based on the collective interest and not on personal interests or those of restricted groups.

TOOLS FOR QUESTIONING REPRESENTATIVES

1. Municipal chambers and legislative sessions

The City Council is the main place to question council members and monitor their performance. Many councils hold sessions open to the public, where citizens can:

- Ask questions and propose demands.
- Watch discussions on bills and public policies.
- Request information directly from councilors.

Practical tip : Check the City Council website or its social media page to check the session calendar and find out if there are any public hearings scheduled.

2. Municipal ombudsman offices

City halls and municipal chambers usually have ombudsman offices, which are official channels for receiving complaints, suggestions and requests for information. This is a direct way to question decisions and ask for clarification on topics such as:

- Expenditure on public works.
- Failures in the provision of services, such as health, education or transport.
- Delays or stoppages of announced projects.

How to use :

- Go to the official website of the city hall or the Municipal Chamber to find the ombudsman channel.
- Send your request clearly, specifying the topic and the required data.
- Keep the protocol to track the progress of your order.

3. Transparency portals

By law, all public bodies are required to disclose detailed information about their actions and expenditures through transparency portals. These portals allow any citizen to consult:

- Contracts signed by the city hall.
- Municipal expenses and revenues.
- Payrolls and salaries of public servants.
- Progress of bids and works.

Practical tip :

- Access your city's transparency portal (search for "Transparency Portal [city name]" on Google).
- Use keywords to find specific information, such as "education," "health," or "constructions."
- If something seems wrong or incomplete, please submit a request to the ombudsman.

4. Access to Information Act (LAI)

The Access to Information Act (Law No. 12,527/2011) guarantees that any citizen can request public information from municipal, state and federal agencies. The Access to Information Act is a powerful tool for investigating decisions and demanding answers on issues of collective interest.

How to use the LAI :

1. Identify what you want to know (example: copy of contracts, justification for a project, amounts paid in a specific bid).
2. Go to the official website of the city hall or the Municipal Chamber and look for the section on requests for access to information.
3. Fill out the form with your request, being as clear and objective as possible.
4. Follow the progress of the order through the protocol.

Deadline for response : The public body has up to 20 working days to respond, and may request an extension of 10 days.

5. Social networks

City halls and city council members often use social media to publicize their actions and interact with the public. These platforms are accessible and direct spaces for asking questions, exposing problems and demanding solutions.

Practical tips :

- Follow the official pages of the city hall, the Municipal Chamber and its representatives.
- Use comments and direct messages to ask questions about specific topics.
- Maintain a respectful but firm tone when stating your demands.

6. Public hearings and consultations

Public hearings are opportunities for the public to express their opinions on important issues, such as changes to urban planning, budget proposals or the implementation of public policies. These meetings are mandatory in many situations and provide a space for citizens to directly participate in the decision-making process.

How to participate :

- Keep an eye out for invitations or announcements of public hearings on official websites and social media.
- Prepare questions or suggestions in advance.
- If possible, bring documents or data to support your participation.

7. Community movements and associations

Community movements and neighborhood associations are excellent tools for strengthening collective demands. Often, a problem faced by one person — such as a lack of public lighting or the need for renovations at a school — is shared by other people in the same region.

How to act in a group :

- Gather a group of residents interested in solving the problem.
- Organize meetings to discuss the best strategies.
- Send letters or collective petitions to the city hall or city council.

STRATEGIES FOR EFFECTIVE COLLECTIONS

1. Be objective and clear

When questioning representatives, avoid generic complaints. Specify what the issue is, why it's important, and what actions you expect to be taken.

> **Bad example** : "The city government doesn't do anything for health."
> **Good example** : "I would like to know why

the health unit in neighborhood X has been without doctors for two weeks. Is there a forecast for normalizing services?"

2. Document your interactions

Always keep records, emails and messages exchanged with representatives or public bodies. This makes it easier to follow up and serves as evidence if the problem is not resolved.

3. Use available data

Before asking questions, consult information on transparency portals or news to support your decision. Presenting concrete data gives more weight to your claim.

4. Keep following

After asking a question, continue to monitor the issue. If you do not receive a response, send a new request or appeal to higher authorities, such as the Public Prosecutor's Office or state and federal agencies.

5. Share the results

If you find answers or solve a problem, share your experience with your community. This encourages others to ask questions and demand action.

PRACTICAL EXAMPLES OF QUESTIONS

- **Education** : "Why doesn't municipal school X have enough materials for its students? What is the budget allocated for this unit?"
- **Works** : "The work on Avenue Y has been delayed for three months. What is the reason for the delay and the new completion date?"
- **Health** : "How many doctors are working at health unit Z? Why has the waiting time for appointments increased?"
- **Transparency** : "I would like to access the contracts signed between the city hall and the company responsible for garbage collection."

Demanding transparency and accountability from mayors and city council members is an exercise in citizenship that strengthens democracy and promotes improvements in public management. Using the available tools, such as ombudsman offices, transparency portals and the Access to Information Law, you can act directly and effectively, helping to build a fairer and better-managed community.

THE POWER OF TRANSPARENCY - HOW TO HOLD POLITICIANS TO ACCOUNT

Transparency is one of the fundamental pillars of a democratic and efficient public administration. When politicians and municipal managers are accountable for their actions, use resources clearly and allow access to public information, citizens gain the opportunity to evaluate, question and influence decisions that impact their lives.

On the other hand, a lack of transparency creates fertile ground for mismanagement, corruption and a weakening of the bond between the population and elected representatives. Demanding transparency is not only a citizen's right, but also a way to promote more responsible and participatory governance.

In this chapter, we will explore the tools and strategies you can use to hold mayors, city council members, and other city managers accountable for their actions and promote transparency in the use of public resources.

WHY IS TRANSPARENCY ESSENTIAL?

Transparency benefits both citizens and public managers. The main reasons for defending it include:

1. **Reduction of corruption and mismanagement** : When there is public access to contracts, tenders and municipal expenditures, it is more difficult for

irregularities to be committed without being noticed.
2. **Strengthening public trust** : Transparency creates an environment of trust, showing that managers are acting in the interest of the community.
3. **Citizen participation** : With clear information, citizens can participate more actively in public debate, making informed demands and suggesting improvements.
4. **Administrative efficiency** : Transparent governments are more likely to use resources responsibly and strategically, as they know that their actions are being monitored.

TOOLS FOR ACCESSING PUBLIC INFORMATION

1. Transparency portals

Transparency portals are mandatory for all municipalities, states and the federal government, as determined by the Access to Information Law (LAI). They are the main tool for verifying how public money is being collected and spent.

Information you can find on transparency portals :

- Municipal budget (revenue and expenditure).
- Contracts signed by the city hall or Municipal Chamber.
- Public tenders and competitions.
- Public servants' salaries.

- Reports on the application of resources in health, education and infrastructure.

How to access :

1. Look for your municipality's transparency portal (a Google search is usually enough).
2. Navigate through the main sections, such as "Expenses", "Income" and "Contracts".
3. Use search filters to find specific information.

Practical tip :

If your city's transparency portal is disorganized or incomplete, send a request for clarification to the city hall or use the Access to Information Law.

2. Access to Information Act (LAI)

The Access to Information Act (LAI) is one of the most powerful tools for ensuring transparency. It allows any citizen to request information about public management, without having to justify the reason for the request.

Examples of information that may be requested :

- Justifications for the delay in public works.
- Detailed documents on signed contracts.
- Budgeting and project planning spreadsheets.

- Information on tenders and administrative processes.

How to make a request through LAI :

1. Access the website of the city hall or Municipal Chamber.
2. e-SIC " (Electronic Citizen Information System) section .
3. Fill out the form with your request, detailing the desired information.
4. Follow the response through the generated protocol.

Response deadline : The administration has up to 20 working days to respond, with the possibility of an extension of another 10 days.

3. Official journals

Official gazettes are public documents where governments publish legal and administrative information, such as decrees, appointments, contracts and bidding results.

How to access :

- Access the municipality's official gazette, usually available online.
- Search for keywords related to the topic you want to investigate.

Practical example :

If a new company has been hired to manage waste collection in your city, you can look in the official gazette for information about the contract and check the agreed terms.

HOW TO INTERPRET PUBLIC ACCOUNTS AND DOCUMENTS

Accessing public information is just the first step; the next is to interpret that data critically to identify potential problems.

1. Compare income and expenses

Check whether the municipality is spending more than it earns. A large deficit may indicate poor management, while consistent surpluses may mean that public money is not being invested adequately in essential services.

2. Analyze contracts and bids

Check for companies that are repeatedly hired, prices that are much higher than the market average, or a lack of competition in bids. These may be signs of favoritism or irregularities.

3. Investment priorities

Compare the city's spending with the population's needs. For example, if the city is facing serious health problems but most of the resources are being allocated to public works, this may indicate a planning failure.

4. Look for irregular patterns

Frequent transfers to the same company or institution without clear justification may be an indication of deviations.

STRATEGIES TO DEMAND MORE TRANSPARENCY

1. Participate in public hearings

Public hearings are moments in which managers and council members present plans and discuss the use of resources with the population. Take advantage of these moments to ask questions, make suggestions and demand transparency.

2. Create or join community groups
Organizing neighborhood groups can increase the strength of your demands. Together, you can send letters, petitions, or even organize demonstrations to demand more transparency.

3. Use social media

City halls and council members often use social media to publicize their actions. Use these channels to question information that is incomplete or unclear.

4. Report irregularities

If you identify possible irregularities, report them to control bodies, such as the Public Prosecutor's Office, Audit Courts or local Comptroller's Offices.

Practical example :

If a project is halted without justification, send a request for information to the city hall and, if you do not receive a response, take the case to the Public Prosecutor's Office.

Practical examples of charging for transparency

- **Budget** : "I would like to know how the budget allocated to health was used this semester. What were the main expenses?"
- **Works** : "The revitalization work on Park X should have been completed in July. What is the reason for the delay and the new delivery forecast?"
- **Contracts** : "I would like to obtain copies of the contracts signed with Company Y over the last two years."
- **Education** : "What investment was made in the maintenance of municipal schools in 2023?"

THE IMPACT OF TRANSPARENCY ON PUBLIC MANAGEMENT

When citizens demand transparency, public managers are pressured to act more responsibly, planning their spending better and ensuring that resources are used for the benefit of the population. Furthermore, transparency reduces the chances of corruption and embezzlement, since politicians' actions are subject to public scrutiny. Cities that prioritize transparency tend to have more efficient administration, with better quality public services and greater community participation in important decisions.

Demanding transparency is one of the most important steps to ensure honest and efficient public management. Using tools such as transparency portals, the Access to Information Law and official gazettes, you can closely monitor the actions of your representatives and demand greater accountability in the administration of your municipality.

MUNICIPAL COUNCILS AND PUBLIC FORUMS - OPPORTUNITIES FOR PARTICIPATION

Municipal councils and public forums are spaces created to allow the population to actively participate in decisions about public policies. These mechanisms ensure that citizens, representatives of organizations and authorities can discuss, plan and monitor actions that directly impact the community, such as investments in health, education, transportation and culture.

Participating in these spaces is an opportunity to exercise your role as a citizen, influencing decisions that shape the future of the municipality and demanding transparency and accountability from public managers. In this chapter, you will learn what municipal councils are, how public forums work, and how to effectively get involved in these processes.

WHAT ARE MUNICIPAL COUNCILS?

Municipal councils are collegiate bodies that bring together representatives of civil society, local government and, in some cases, private entities, with the aim of discussing and deciding on public policies in specific areas. They are regulated by municipal laws and aim to promote dialogue between the population and the public administration.

MAIN CHARACTERISTICS OF MUNICIPAL COUNCILS:

- **Equal composition**: Generally, councils are composed of representatives of public authorities and civil society in similar proportions.
- **Deliberative or consultative function**: Some councils have the power to make decisions (deliberative), while others only issue opinions and recommendations (consultative).
- **Thematic focus**: Each council addresses a specific area, such as health, education, housing, environment or transport.

Examples of municipal councils:

1. **Municipal Health Council**
   - Supervises and monitors the actions and expenses of the health sector.
   - Participates in the preparation of the municipal health plan.
2. **Municipal Education Council**
   - Analyzes educational policy proposals.
   - Monitors the application of resources in the area of education.
3. **Municipal Environmental Council**
   - Evaluates environmental impact projects.
   - Proposes actions for the preservation and recovery of the environment.
4. **Guardianship Council**
   - It works to protect and guarantee the rights of children and adolescents.

HOW TO PARTICIPATE IN MUNICIPAL COUNCILS

1. Identify the councils that exist in your municipality

Check the city hall website or contact the municipal departments to find out which councils are active and in which areas you can participate.

2. Understand the rules of composition

Each council has its own rules of membership. In many cases, you must be a member of a civil society organization or participate in an election or nomination process to become a councilor.

3. Attend open meetings

Even if you are not an official board member, many board meetings are open to the public. Attending these meetings is a great way to follow the discussions and make suggestions.

4. Follow the minutes and decisions

Meeting minutes are often posted online or available upon request. Reading these documents helps you understand the decisions made and plan your participation.

WHAT ARE PUBLIC FORUMS?

Public forums are meetings organized to discuss specific topics with the participation of government and society representatives. Unlike councils, which have a permanent structure, forums are held on an ad hoc basis, usually to discuss urgent issues or important projects.

Examples of public forums:

- Discussions on the Municipal Master Plan.
- Debates on participatory budgeting.
- Thematic forums to discuss urban mobility, basic sanitation or culture.

Public forums allow citizens to present their demands, ask questions and propose solutions directly to public managers, acting as a bridge between the community and the government.

HOW TO PARTICIPATE IN PUBLIC FORUMS

1. Pay attention to invitations and announcements

Public forums are usually announced on the city's website, social media, or local media outlets. Keep an eye on these channels to find out when they will take place.

2. Prepare in advance

Before participating in a forum, find out about the topic that will be discussed. Consult data and reports related to the subject and prepare questions or suggestions to present during the meeting.

3. Use the space to question and propose

Forums are a unique opportunity to engage directly with administrators and other citizens. Use the space to voice concerns and suggest solutions that meet the needs of the community.

4. Track the results

After the forum, check whether the proposals presented were recorded and whether there will be follow-up or implementation of the suggestions made.

Tips for being an active and effective participant

1. **Get informed in advance**
   Before attending a meeting or forum, research the topic, read related documents and understand the main issues at stake.
2. **Be clear and objective**
   When expressing your opinion or questioning something, be direct and present arguments based on data and facts. This increases the chances that your contribution will be taken seriously.
3. **Organize in a group**
   Participating in councils and forums together with

other people who share the same demands strengthens your voice and makes your demands harder to ignore.

4. **Document everything**
   Write down the main points discussed, the decisions made and the promises made by managers. This will help you to monitor developments and demand results in the future.

5. **Maintain respect**
   Even in situations of disagreement, maintain a respectful tone. This demonstrates maturity and increases your credibility as a participant.

THE IMPACT OF PUBLIC COUNCILS AND FORUMS ON THE COMMUNITY

When the population actively participates in councils and forums, public managers are pressured to consider the real demands of the community and make more transparent and inclusive decisions. In addition, these spaces help prevent the misuse of resources and mismanagement, since social control makes government actions more visible and open to question.

Through these mechanisms, the population has the opportunity to directly influence public policies, promoting improvements in essential areas such as health, education and infrastructure.

PRACTICAL EXAMPLES OF SUCCESSFUL PARTICIPATION

- **Participatory Master Plan** : In several cities, public forums to review the Master Plan led to the inclusion of residents' demands, such as the preservation of green areas and the improvement of public transportation.
- **Participatory Budget** : In municipalities that adopt participatory budgeting, the population decides where part of the resources will be applied, prioritizing works or services that are important to the community.
- **Municipal Health Council** : Citizens who participate in health councils often identify flaws in the system and contribute to improving care in municipal clinics and hospitals.

Municipal councils and public forums are powerful tools for strengthening citizen participation and ensuring that public policies meet the real needs of the population. By getting involved in these spaces, you not only exercise your rights, but also actively contribute to building a more democratic, transparent and efficient public administration.

LOCAL ORGANIZATION AND ACTIVISM - UNITING THE COMMUNITY TO DEMAND IMPROVEMENT

When people in a community come together to discuss issues and find solutions, they create a collective impact that is far greater than they could achieve individually. Community organizing and local activism are powerful ways to pressure policymakers, drive change, and ensure that people's needs are met.

In this chapter, we will explore how to form and strengthen community groups, plan collective actions, and maximize the impact of their demands on public officials. We will also discuss examples of successful activism, showing how community members coming together can transform neighborhoods and cities.

WHAT IS COMMUNITY ORGANIZATION?

Community organizing is the process of bringing together people who share common problems or interests to seek collective solutions. It can be formal, such as neighborhood associations and community councils, or informal, such as WhatsApp groups or casual get-togethers to discuss local issues.

Community organization goals :

- Identify problems and priorities.
- Propose collective solutions and create action plans.

- Put pressure on public and private authorities.
- Promote the well-being and quality of life of the community.

Community organizing is particularly effective because it reflects the real concerns of local people, creating genuine demands that public managers cannot ignore.

STEPS TO ORGANIZING YOUR COMMUNITY

1. Identify priority problems

Gather residents together to discuss the main problems in the area. These could be poor sanitation, security issues, inefficient public transportation, or a lack of recreational facilities. List the most pressing issues and choose one or two to focus on initially.

2. Form an active group

Identify people who are interested in actively participating in discussions and actions. A small but engaged group can be more effective than a large number of uncommitted participants.

Practical tip : Use social media, flyers or informal invitations to attract members. WhatsApp or Telegram groups can facilitate communication.

3. Create a basic structure

Define roles within the group, such as one person responsible for communicating with authorities, another for organizing meetings, and another for publicizing actions. A well-defined structure helps avoid confusion and increases efficiency.

4. Research and document information

Before filing a complaint with the authorities, collect data about the problem. Conduct research, take photos, record complaints from residents, and, if possible, obtain statistics or official reports. These documents will strengthen your argument.

5. Set clear goals

Determine what changes you want to achieve and what steps are needed to achieve them. Break down the goals into smaller, achievable targets to keep the group motivated and focused.

Practical example :

If the goal is to build a new daycare center, goals might include:

- Gather 100 signatures of support from the community.
- Request information about the budget allocated to education.

- Organize a meeting with the municipal secretary of education.

6. Engage the larger community

Even if not all residents can actively participate in meetings, let them know about the group's activities and ask for their support. Flyers, open meetings, and social media campaigns are great ways to get more people involved.

LOCAL ACTIVISM STRATEGIES

1. Petitions and petitions

One of the simplest and most effective ways to mobilize the community is to organize petitions or petitions. These demonstrate the population's support for a specific demand and can be delivered to the appropriate authorities or agencies.

Practical tip : Use digital tools like Change.org to expand your petition's reach and attract more supporters.

2. Meetings with authorities

Organize meetings with council members, mayors or municipal secretaries to present your demands. Show that the group is well organized and prepared, with clear information and proposed solutions.

3. Community events

Organize community outreach, peaceful protests, marches, or cultural events to draw attention to the issue and engage more people. These events also help to raise awareness of the cause in the media.

4. Pressure on social media

Use platforms like Facebook, Instagram, and Twitter to publicize community issues and tag the authorities responsible. The more engagement you have online, the harder it will be for managers to ignore the demand.

Practical example : Post photos and videos of streets without lighting or schools in poor condition, tagging the city hall and the councilors responsible. Use hashtags to increase reach.

5. Partnerships with NGOs and experts

Seek support from non-governmental organizations, universities, or experts in the field in question. They can offer resources, technical guidance, and even legal support to strengthen your cause.

6. Local media coverage

Contact local newspapers, blogs, or radio stations to publicize the issues facing the community and the actions taken by the group. Good media coverage can increase pressure on authorities.

EXAMPLES OF SUCCESSFUL LOCAL ACTIVISM

1. **Revitalizing public squares**
   In many cities, community groups have organized to revitalize abandoned squares and parks, either through collective efforts or by pressuring the city government to provide resources and maintenance.
2. **Improvements in public transportation**
   Communities that faced problems with bus schedules or routes achieved significant changes by mobilizing residents, organizing petitions, and talking to transportation companies and municipal authorities.
3. **Environmental protection**
   Community groups have already prevented the construction of projects that threatened green areas by mobilizing the population, seeking support from NGOs and pressuring public managers based on environmental laws.
4. **School Renovations**
   Parents and residents in one area pressured the city government to renovate schools in poor condition, using photos, accounts from teachers and students, and press coverage to highlight the problem.

TIPS FOR KEEPING THE GROUP MOTIVATED

1. **Celebrate small achievements**
   Even if the results are gradual, celebrate each step forward. This keeps the group motivated and focused on the bigger goal.
2. **Maintain clear communication**
   Regularly update participants on actions taken and next steps. Use messaging groups, emails, or face-to-face meetings to keep everyone aligned.
3. **Seek partnerships and resources**
   Identify local organizations or businesses that can support the group with material resources or expertise.
4. **Avoid internal divisions**
   Conflicts within the group can weaken the movement. Encourage dialogue and collaboration to resolve differences.
5. **Believe in collective impact**
   Reinforce the importance of unity and collective work to achieve significant changes.

THE IMPACT OF COMMUNITY ORGANIZATION ON PUBLIC MANAGEMENT

When the community organizes itself and acts in an articulated manner, it becomes an agent of change. Public authorities are pressured to act more quickly and responsibly, while the sense of community strengthens the bond between residents and promotes a more participatory and democratic environment.

Well-organized community groups are living examples that power is not only in the hands of public managers, but also in the hands of the population.

Local organizing and activism are essential tools for driving real change in your community. By joining forces, engaging residents, and using effective lobbying strategies, you can turn local issues into priorities for government officials.

USING SOCIAL MEDIA FOR TRANSPARENT COLLECTION

Social media has transformed the way people communicate, organize, and demand change. Today, platforms like Facebook, Instagram, Twitter, WhatsApp, and TikTok are not only spaces for socializing, but also powerful tools for community mobilization and demanding transparency and accountability from public officials.

In the local context, where citizens and representatives are more closely connected, social media offers a unique opportunity to expose problems, amplify demands, and pressure authorities to act. In this chapter, we will explore how to use social media strategically and effectively to promote improvements in your city and demand transparency from public officials.

WHY USE SOCIAL MEDIA FOR COLLECTION?

Social media offers important advantages for those who want to demand transparency and change:

1. **Wide and fast reach** : A post can reach thousands of people in just a few minutes, including residents, journalists and the authorities themselves.
2. **Ease of access** : Anyone with a cell phone or computer can participate, regardless of where they are .

3. **Interactivity** : It is possible to dialogue directly with public managers, mark official profiles and engage other citizens.
4. **Public pressure** : When an issue is widely shared, it gains more visibility, forcing authorities to act to avoid damaging their image.

STRATEGIES FOR USING SOCIAL MEDIA TO DEMAND TRANSPARENCY

1. Identify the problem and document it

Before posting anything, make sure you have clear and accurate information about the issue you want to address. Take photos, record videos, or gather documents that help illustrate the issue.

Practical example :

If the public lighting on a street is poor, take photos of the location at night, showing the darkness, and record how this impacts the safety of residents.

2. Write clear and objective messages

When posting on social media, use simple, direct language to explain the issue and what you hope will be done. Include essential information such as the location and impact of the issue on the community.

Example of an effective post:

"Rua das Flores has been without public lighting for weeks. The lack of light has caused insecurity and there have been two robberies recently. We ask that @PrefeituraDeExemplo take urgent measures. #PublicLighting #SafetyForAll"

3. Use strategic hashtags

Hashtags help to expand the reach of your post, making it easier for other people with the same issue to find it and engage. Create hashtags specific to your topic or use popular ones.

Example:

- #TransparencyNow
- #HealthInTheNeighborhood
- #WorkStopped
- #ResponsibleManagement

4. Tag official profiles and public figures

Identify the profiles of the city hall, municipal departments, councilors and other responsible authorities and tag them in your posts. This increases the chance of your message being seen by those who can solve the problem.

Practical example:

"@PrefeitoDeExemplo , the work on the square in neighborhood X has been on hold for months. Residents want to know when it will be finished. #PraçaDoBairroX"

5. Engage the community

Share your post in resident groups on WhatsApp, Facebook or Telegram, encouraging others to comment , like and share. The greater the engagement, the greater the visibility of the issue.

Practical tip : Organize "mobilization days," where all group members post about the same issue at the same time, increasing pressure.

6. Tell real stories

Stories from people affected by the problem make the post more impactful and generate greater empathy. Include testimonials from residents or record everyday situations to illustrate how the issue affects the community.

Example :

"Dona Maria, 70 years old, lives in neighborhood X and depends on the local health center for consultations. Due to the lack of doctors, she has to wait months for care. @PrefeituraDeExemplo, this needs to change! #HealthForAll"

7. Post updates and results

After making an initial post, keep the community informed of developments. If there is a response from the authorities, share it with everyone and continue to push for a solution until it is implemented.

SPECIFIC TOOLS FOR SOCIAL NETWORKS

Facebook

- Ideal for creating community groups and sharing detailed information.
- Use live streaming to discuss local issues and engage other residents.

Instagram

- Visual posts and stories are effective at highlighting issues with photos and videos.
- Use polls and question boxes in stories to engage your audience.

Twitter

- Great for direct dialogues with authorities and journalists.

- Take advantage of the trends local topics to give more visibility to the issue.

WhatsApp and Telegram

- Create specific groups to mobilize residents and share updates.
- Send direct messages to local leaders, such as councilors or secretaries.

TikTok

- Short, creative videos can be used to draw attention to serious issues in a light-hearted and impactful way.
- Use popular songs or trends to expand your reach.

CAUTION WHEN USING SOCIAL MEDIA FOR COLLECTION

1. **Check your facts before posting**
   Make sure the information you're sharing is true. Posting something that's incorrect can hurt your credibility and make it harder to collect on it in the future.
2. **Maintain respect**
   Avoid personal attacks, insults, or insults when addressing authorities. A respectful tone increases the chances of being taken seriously.
3. **Avoid over-posting**
   Be strategic. Posting about the same issue too

many times in a short space of time can lead to loss of engagement or being blocked by official profiles.

4. **Protect your privacy**
Avoid sharing personal information, such as your address or phone number, in public posts.

5. **Report inappropriate practices**
If your post is the target of attacks or offensive comments, use social media tools to report and block abusive users.

SUCCESSFUL EXAMPLES OF USING SOCIAL NETWORKS

1. **Street repair effort**
A group of residents used Instagram to post photos of potholed streets and tag the city government. After the post went viral, the problem was fixed in less than two weeks.

2. **School reopening**
Parents of students used Facebook to organize a protest against the closure of a municipal school. The posts gained attention from local media and forced the city government to reopen the school.

3. **Monitoring public works**
Residents of a neighborhood monitored the progress of a construction project and posted regular updates on Twitter, tagging the authorities in charge. The constant pressure accelerated the project's completion.

THE IMPACT OF SOCIAL NETWORKS ON PUBLIC MANAGEMENT

Social media has changed the dynamics between citizens and public officials. Issues that could previously be ignored now gain visibility and generate almost immediate pressure. In addition, platforms allow citizens to connect with each other, forming support and mobilization networks that amplify their voices.

Managers who value transparency use social media as tools to engage with the public, present results, and respond to demands. On the other hand, citizens who use these platforms strategically can accelerate solutions and strengthen democratic participation.

Social media is an accessible and powerful tool for demanding transparency, exposing issues, and mobilizing communities to find solutions. By using it strategically and respectfully, you can amplify your voice and ensure that your community's demands reach the appropriate authorities.

30 DAYS TO EVALUATE AND DEMAND ACTION FROM JOURNALISM AND LOCAL REPRESENTATIVES

Now that you've learned how to identify questionable journalistic practices, demand transparency from your representatives, and use tools like city councils, social media, and community organizing, it's time to put all of this into practice. This 30-day plan was created to help you critically evaluate local journalism, monitor the actions of politicians in your city, and start making structured and effective demands.

Each week will be dedicated to a specific area, with daily tasks and clear goals. By the end of the 30 days, you will have developed a more active and conscious approach to what is happening in your city and will be prepared to demand real change.

WEEK 1: INITIAL LOCAL MEDIA MONITORING

Objective: To identify patterns in local journalism and evaluate the quality of the information published.

> **Day 1: Make a list of the main local vehicles**
> - Identify print newspapers, websites, blogs, and radio or TV programs that cover news about your city.
> - Follow these outlets on social media to receive regular updates.
>
> **Day 2: Assess the tone of the headlines**

- Read a day's headlines and see if they are sensationalist in tone or reflect the actual content of the story.
- Ask yourself: Does the title inform or manipulate?

Day 3: Analyze the diversity of sources
- Choose a recently published article and see how many sources were cited.
- Ask yourself: Do these sources represent different points of view?

Day 4: Identify recurring themes
- List the most discussed topics in recent days, such as education, health, transportation or security.
- Check whether these topics are relevant to the community or whether there is a pattern of favoring certain figures or institutions.

Day 5: Record omissions
- Note if there are important issues in your city that are not being covered by the local media.
- Compare it to what is being discussed on social media or among residents.

WEEK 2: IDENTIFYING RELEASES AND COPIED MATERIALS

Objective: Recognize the influence of official releases on local journalism and identify sponsored content.

Day 6: Research repeated subjects
- Compare news from different local media outlets and see if there are any very similar

stories. This may indicate the use of unedited press releases.

Day 7: Observe the official language
- Read carefully an article about an action by the city hall or an authority.
- Ask yourself: Does the text sound like an advertisement? Does it use complimentary adjectives or unexplained technical terms?

Day 8: Check for criticism or counterpoints
- Choose an article about a public project and see if it presents criticism or divergent opinions.
- Record when the material appears partial or incomplete.

Day 9: Compare with official sources
- Visit the city hall's website or social media and see if any article published by local media is identical to an official release.
- Note examples of " copy and paste journalism."

Day 10: Identify sponsored content
- Read articles that mention companies or projects and look for signs of sponsorship, such as exaggerated praise or lack of criticism.

WEEK 3: TREND WATCHING AND OPINION COLUMNS

Objective: To assess the impartiality of columnists and identify trends in journalistic coverage.

Day 11: Analyze an opinion column

- Choose a recently published column and see if the author presents well-founded arguments or just personal opinions.
- Check if the text clearly favors an authority or group.

Day 12: Compare columns from different vehicles
- Read columns on the same topic in different outlets and see if there is a contrast in the opinions presented.
- Record which outlets appear to be most critical or aligned with the government.

Day 13: Identify trends in stories
- Notice if there are figures or institutions that receive predominantly positive or negative coverage.
- Ask yourself: Does this trend reflect the facts or does it indicate favoritism?

Day 14: Assess the impact of columns on public debate
- See how the columns discuss important topics, such as budget, public works or scandals.
- Ask yourself: Do these opinions help people understand the topic or do they just reinforce specific narratives?

Day 15: Search for column omissions
- Note whether there are public figures or political parties that are never mentioned in the columns, even when involved in relevant topics.

WEEK 4: COLLECTION AND TRANSPARENCY

Objective: Start holding local representatives accountable and demanding more transparency and accountability.

Day 16: Choose a relevant topic
- Identify a major problem in your city, such as a delayed construction project, a lack of doctors, or transportation problems.

Day 17: Research official information
- Use the transparency portal, official gazettes or the Access to Information Law to obtain data on the chosen topic.

Day 18: Post on social media
- Share information about the issue on your social networks, using relevant photos, data and hashtags.
- Tag official profiles of the city hall, councilors or responsible secretaries.

Day 19: Send formal inquiries
- Use the ombudsman's office at the city hall or city council to send questions or complaints about the chosen problem.
- Keep the protocol and monitor the progress of the request.

Day 20: Start a petition or mobilize your community
- Gather like-minded residents and create a petition or plan a meeting with local officials to discuss the issue.

WEEK 5: MONITORING RESULTS

Objective: Assess the impact of your actions and plan the next steps.

Day 21: Follow the responses
- See if authorities have responded to your posts or formal requests.
- If there is no response, send a new request or use social media to reinforce the demand.

Day 22: Compare social media engagement
- Analyze the reach of posts made about the chosen problem.
- Evaluate the impact of community mobilization and see if more people started discussing the topic.

Day 23: Post updates
- Share the authorities' responses (or lack thereof) on social media.
- Keep pushing until concrete action is taken.

Day 24: Check for changes in media coverage
- See if the topic gained space in the local media after your mobilization.
- Note if there have been changes in approach or inclusion of more critical voices.

Day 25: Plan next steps
- Meet with your community or advocacy group to evaluate results and discuss new strategies.

In the last 5 days, use what you learned during the month to build a routine of monitoring, accountability, and citizen participation. Here are the goals for the final days of the plan:

Days 26 to 30:
1. **Strengthen your support network** : Continue engaging the community and connect with others interested in demanding improvements for the city.
2. **Monitor the actions of local representatives** : Assess whether the promises made during your collections are being fulfilled.
3. **Share good practices** : Share the positive results you have achieved with your mobilization and encourage others to do the same.
4. **Keep demanding transparency** : Use the tools learned throughout this book to demand more accountability and participation from government and local media.

This action plan is a starting point for transforming your relationship with local journalism and its representatives. By adopting a critical and active stance, you not only strengthen your voice as a citizen, but also contribute to building a more just, informed and participatory society.

Remember: change starts with small but consistent actions. Your city needs engaged citizens like you to grow in a more transparent and accountable way.

AN ACTIVE AND INFORMED CITIZEN TRANSFORMS HIS COMMUNITY

Throughout this book, we explore how to identify problematic practices in local journalism, recognize biased content, and demand greater transparency and accountability from mayors and city council members. More than a guide to understanding the behind-the-scenes of journalism and public management, this work is an invitation for you to take an active role in your city, transforming the relationship between society and its representatives.

The power of a well-informed and engaged community is immeasurable. When citizens question, demand and actively participate, authorities are pressured to act more ethically, efficiently and responsibly. Furthermore, the presence of an independent and critical local press strengthens democracy, ensuring that all sides of a story are heard.

This journey doesn't end here. Transformation requires continuity, consistency, and unity. You now have the tools you need to take action and influence the future of your community.

THE POWER OF THE INDIVIDUAL AND THE COLLECTIVE

Meaningful change starts with small steps. One individual who questions a decision or exposes a problem can inspire others to join in, creating a movement that echoes throughout the city. With the knowledge gained in this book, you will be better prepared to:

1. **Identify and combat misinformation** : You know how to recognize fake news and biased narratives, protecting yourself from manipulation.
2. **Charge based on facts** : By understanding the roles and limits of mayors and councilors, your demands will be more well-founded and targeted.
3. **Demand transparency** : Using tools such as transparency portals and the Access to Information Act, you can monitor and oversee public management.
4. **Mobilize your community** : Organizing around common causes is the foundation for significant achievements.
5. **Strengthen the local press** : By supporting independent and ethical media outlets, you help preserve journalism that serves the public interest.

NEXT STEPS: CHANGE STARTS NOW

As you apply the knowledge you've gained, remember: the key to success lies in continuity and collaboration. Here are some suggestions for getting started after finishing this book:

1. Monitor local journalism

Continue to analyze how your city's media outlets cover the news, identifying questionable practices and valuing ethical and balanced journalism.

2. Follow up with your representatives

Find out who the councilors and mayor of your city are, follow their actions and use official channels to make frequent demands.

3. Start a discussion in your community

Share what you learn with friends, family, and neighbors. Together, you can create a movement to address local issues.

4. Support independent journalism

Subscribe, donate or share content produced by independent media outlets. They are essential for honest public debate.

5. Be an example of active citizenship

Participate in public forums, city councils, or community meetings. Your presence makes a difference and inspires others to get involved.

Being an active and informed citizen is more than a right; it is a responsibility. It is through small actions, such as questioning a biased article or demanding answers from a councilor, that we build a more just and democratic society.

You have the power to transform your city and strengthen transparency and truth. This book is just the beginning of a journey that, with your participation, can result in a more informed, engaged, and prosperous community.

Change is in your hands. Are you ready to act?

As we turn the final page of this journey together, I sincerely hope that the lessons shared here have touched your heart and opened up new perspectives. If this book has brought you any value, I kindly ask that you take a moment to leave a review on Amazon. Your words not only help me grow and improve my craft, but they also guide other readers in their quest for knowledge and inspiration. Your feedback is a valuable gift, both to me and to the community of readers seeking transformative stories. I sincerely thank you for sharing this journey with me, and I hope we can meet again in the pages of a new adventure.

REGINALDO OSNILDO

Hello, I'm Reginaldo Osnildo, an author and innovator in the areas of sales, technology, and communication strategies. My experience ranges from academia, as a professor and researcher at the University of Southern Santa Catarina, to practice as a strategist at Grupo Catarinense de Rádios. With a PhD in sales narratives and digital convergence, and a master's degree in storytelling and social imaginary, I bring to my readers a unique fusion of theory and practice. My goal is to provide knowledge in simple, practical, and didactic language, encouraging direct application in personal and professional life.

Yours sincerely

Reginaldo Osnildo

www.ingramcontent.com/pod-product-compliance
Lightning Source LLC
Chambersburg PA
CBHW052146220526
45471CB00004B/1543